Paul Duncan

The Pocket Essential

NOIR FICTION

Gerald Nor...
Dashiell...

GW00383878

www.pocketessentials.com

First published in Great Britain 2000, revised 2003 by
Pocket Essentials, P O Box 394, Harpenden, Herts, AL5 1XJ, UK

Distributed in the USA by Trafalgar Square Publishing,
PO Box 257, Howe Hill Road, North Pomfret, Vermont 05053

Copyright © Paul Duncan 2000, 2003
Editor: Paul Duncan

A CIP catalogue record for this book is available from the British Library.

ISBN 1-903047-11-0

2 4 6 8 10 9 7 5 3

Book typeset by Wordsmith Solutions Ltd
Printed and bound by Cox & Wyman

for Claude

Acknowledgements

Thanks to Victor Berch, Richard Bleiler, Etienne Borgers, Steve Holland, Claude Mesplede and Lynn Munroe for their help with research. As ever my thanks to my Roman Blanc, Claude.

CONTENTS

"A man who has become conscious of the absurd is forever bound to it. A man devoid of hope and is conscious of being so has ceased to belong to the future"

from *Notebooks* by Albert Camus

'She felt a comfortable solidarity with the big company of the voluntary dead'

from *Big Blonde* by Dorothy Parker

'There is nothing escapist about the black novel whatever. The writer cannot even escape himself in it; the black novel is the novel in which escape is shut off'

Derek Raymond

'All great literature is depressing'

Charles Willeford

Noir Fiction: Dark Highways

I am not well. By that I mean that I am sick. Emotionally, physically, psychologically. The world is horrible. I wake in the morning, in my room, a small box at the end of a cement garden, and I look out at the black walls and grey skies, and I think myself better off in my room. Why do I need to go out there? What can I find out there that will make my life better? People? People are obnoxious, smelly, violent, impolite slabs of meat that travel from one place to another like ants following the invisible trails of their dead ancestors. They can teach me nothing - they do not know the things I know. No. I shall stay in my room and I will become pure. I will expel the filth that is within me, vomit up all the bad thoughts, the lifetime of programming that society imprints on my brain, and cleanse myself. I am not alone in my ideas. Many other writers think like me. Even in my putrid little room, I can hear the doubt in your minds. You want proof, you shall have proof. I will write it all down for you, so that you can see the world as it really is...

Noir is all those things we fear in the back of our minds, the parts of ourselves we want to block out because they make us feel uneasy. Noir doesn't always have pat solutions and attractive people, doesn't spoon-feed safe fantasies into drooling mouths. Noir drags you screaming and kicking through all sorts of hell before reaching some sort of unsatisfactory ending. It's not something that many people can take.

Noir requires emotional commitment from the reader. The reader must be prepared to expose themselves to thoughts and feelings they'd rather not think or feel, and that's a hard thing to ask. At best, you can learn something about people and yourself. It all depends upon how much of the Noir you are willing to recognise in yourself.

Noir is often associated with the crime, detective and thriller genres because they give ample opportunity for you to gaze into the minds of bad, dark people on the edge of society. There is little chance of these characters invading your secure privacy. This is the fallacy. These people are actually you. They live and express your secret desires, weaknesses, and motives. It is safer for the character to live for you than for you to admit your dark side to yourself. The crime, mystery, thriller and detective clichés are a code to protect you, a wall you build to stop yourself from being hurt.

That's what *you* think....

Reading Noir is not a good experience. By that, I mean that when pouring over the black and white text of a Hard-Boiled or Action or Romance or Crime or Horror novel, there is a certain vicarious experience which leads to pleasure. You feel uplifted and alive. You wish to share the experience, the frisson, with your neighbour. After finishing a Noir novel, one is more likely to look upon their neighbour - if not with suspicion, then certainly with caution. Despite its name, Noir Fiction - or the Black Novel as some call it - is more likely to muddy the moral waters of our life rather than to make us see things clearly in Black and White.

Since it came into the English language in the mid-1980s, the word Noir has been used and abused. During the 1990s it became a buzzword, a designer label of a peculiar type of fiction that has black comedy apparel but rarely a heart of darkness. This has resulted in Tart Noir, Tartan Noir, Seaside Noir, Surf Noir and Country Noir among others. No doubt a book proclaiming itself part of the new Black Noir movement will soon find itself on the shelves.

I can wait.

Let me make it clear, from the outset, what this book is about. Noir is not a kind of macho Hard-Boiled fiction where Tough Guys pass moral judgement on an immoral society. Noir is about the weak-minded, the losers, the bottom-feeders, the obsessives, the compulsives and the psychopaths. Noir is not about the people standing on the edge of the abyss looking in, but about the people in it, forever writhing, aware of the pain, aware of the future pain to come. The character(s) must suffer/confront the darkness inside them. Whether they live or die is immaterial - the quest into this heart of darkness is the thing.

Definition

The word Hard-Boiled first appeared in cooking recipes of the 1730s to refer to hard-boiled eggs. Mark Twain used it in 1886 to refer to rigid grammatical rules and by 1903, it was used to mean hard or stiff clothing such as the hat of a cowboy or the suits of travelling salesmen. By the end of World War One, it was commonly used to describe a rigid person, one who would not take a chance or relax a rule. It soon came to mean a person who was cynical, stoic and emotionally untouchable - the antithesis of Noir characters who are in constant pain and will tell the reader about it at the drop of a hat (hard-boiled or not).

In America, the emotionally untouchable man was born in the popular myth of the American cowboy. He is a wanderer, a free spirit. It's hokum of course but the myth evolved - the trail turned into the railroad, and later into the highway. The metaphor of travel was used as a device to describe and discover America. In the hands of Jack London and Jim Tully, the cowboy turned into the adventurer and the hobo. During the Depression, socialist writers like John Steinbeck led us down dust-bowl roads telling us about the bitter grapes of wrath, telling it like it was. Writers travelled the highways and byways, going walkabout to discover the world and themselves, to put themselves in touch with the masses, with society. In Britain, writers like George Orwell turned hobo to find out about the world they lived in.

Some authors then began to use Private Investigators to comment on society. The earliest known PI story is *The Black Sleuth* by John E Bruce, which was serialised in *McGirt's Reader* from 1907 to 1909. However, the foremost exponent of the Hard-Boiled story was the *Black Mask* pulp magazine. The December 1922 issue featured the first Hard-Boiled stories: *The False Burton Combs* by Carroll John Daly and *The Road Home* by Peter Collinson (aka Dashiell Hammett).

Dashiell Hammett and other American pulp writers of the 1920s wrote down what they heard on the streets. They used the voices of ordinary people for the first time. Also, from 1926, when Captain Joseph T Shaw became editor of *Black Mask*, the style and content of the Hard-Boiled school was gradually refined to be as close as possible to Hammett's example. The writers found the wisecracking street slang that existed in the alleyways and gutters of America, then combined these words with tight plots and crusading heroes, to craft violent, moral, asexual stories which had a veneer of reality. The restrained 'realism' cloaked a multitude of detectives, criminals and grifters in their sometimes unbelievable, and mostly salacious adventures. The more literary American writers of the time, like Ernest Hemingway (*A Farewell To Arms* (1929)), William Faulkner (*Sanctuary* (1931)), and John O'Hara (*Appointment In Samarra* (1934)), also began using the American language popularised by the Hard-Boiled writers.

Dashiell Hammett (1894-1961), a former Pinkerton detective - he knew a man who stole a Ferris wheel - created the Continental Op and Sam Spade who appeared in the novels *Red Harvest* (1929) and *The Maltese Falcon* (1930) respectively. The frightening thing about these 'heroes' is that they were detached observers of people with money and power. Their emotions seemed to have little effect on their intellectual actions. They were cold people who acted as judge, jury and executioner.

There are many other tough *Black Mask* writers who followed Hammett's tradition, including Paul Cain (1902-1966) (*Fast One* (1933), *Seven Slayers* (1946)), and Raoul Whitfield (1898-1945) (*Green Ice* (1930), *Death In A Bowl* (1932)). However, Raymond Chandler (1888-1959) was the writer who changed the Hard-Boiled protagonist, and most influenced all subsequent Hard-Boiled writers. Chandler came to crime writing late in life but he brought a lyrical approach to the genre which served to romanticise the tough 'tecs, especially his own Philip Marlowe (*The Big Sleep* (1939)). His literary embellishments served to move the reader one more step away from the terror that is death, murder and betrayal. He also refined the wisecracking voice which became the model upon which 1000 private eyes have been launched.

At the time, and for many years, these authors were known as Tough Guy or Hard-Boiled writers. (There was even a *Hardboiled* magazine which ran for 5 issues from October 1936 to February 1937.) Hard-Boiled has become the most common description. However, I intend to show that there is another literature which is present within some Hard-Boiled stories, and is also running parallel with it. This is Noir Fiction.

The history of the word Noir is not as straightforward as you might expect.

Noir is a French word which means the colour black, and can express the gloom and sorrow of mourning. Noir became known internationally through the game of Roulette where it appears on the table opposite Rouge (Red). In the game, they are the only colours upon which you could bet, which gave you a 50% chance of winning, and a 50% chance to lose. (A Noir Fiction book uses this idea in its title: *You Play The Black And The Red Comes Up* (1938) by Richard Hallas (aka Eric Knight).) Even then, all is not what it seems because the wheel also contains the numbers 0 and 00, which means that the odds are stacked against you even more. Gamblers know that Roulette is a suckers game because there is no skill involved - it is all down to pure luck. The only reason to play Roulette is if you want to lose.

The French coined the phrase Roman Noir (Black Novel) to describe the Gothic or Terror novels which first appeared in the second half of the 18th Century in England. These were novels or stories about the dark side of life. They mixed several aesthetic influences (the sentimental, the sublime, rococo, sepulchral poetry), different tastes (attraction for the past, the gothic style, a change of scenery) and gave nature a sense of waste and desolation. Often supernatural and moral elements were added to allow the author to describe excess and frenzy, and to write stories which demonstrate the power and vanity of evil, of misery and the victory of innocence.

The Gothic novel, through the use of the supernatural and the fantastic, is a perversion of the aesthetics of the Sublime, being obsessed with confinement and presenting the past as a pathological determination. (The concept of the Sublime was put forward in 1674. There the emphasis in writing (mainly poetry and essays since the novel form was then in its infancy) was on obscurity, power, darkness, solitude and vastness. Nature was the source of the Sublime. Most Noir Fictions of the 20th Century are decidedly anti-nature since they are set almost exclusively within the city.)

The first Gothic novel was *The Castle Of Otranto* (1764) by Horace Walpole, which begins with the death of a groom during his wedding and escalates into supernatural tale featuring mistaken identity and doomed lovers. (Anybody familiar with the work of 20th Century writer Cornell Woolrich will recognise these themes within his work.) This type of novel became known as a Gothic novel because they were usually set in a medieval castle, convent, monastery or an ancient building. In fact, the titles often referred to a tomb, a castle, a convent, a secret passage or a forest. However, this origin was soon forgotten and Gothic came to represent 'the horror within.'

Roman Noir told of the misfortunes of virtue and the havoc wrought by love, and contrasted these against a background of order and morality (as represented by the setting). The conventions of the Roman Noir (playing with extreme feelings, mixture of eroticism, religious references and satanism), its geography and space (foreign countries, castles, cellars, secret passages), its often naïve usage of references to the supernatural, and its emphasis on horror have meant that the genre has been associated with a literature of rupture and subversion.

The Roman Noir investigates the past of its characters to determine what horrific experiences they underwent to pervert their moral character. Thus, just as the orderly settings (castle) reveal their chaos when looked at in detail (dungeon, secret passages), so do the characters. As an extension of this, it reveals the chaotic/unpredictable beast/barbarian within an orderly society. However, to reveal this to the audience, the author must adopt an unrealistic writing form.

As early as the 18th century, the Roman Noir was used to deal with social taboos through comparison of the present and the past, morality and immorality, open space and confinement, reality and unreality. Despite the conventional conclusions of most of the early Gothic novels, the terror element remained an integral part of it - the idea was not to show the world as completely evil but to create doubt about the future because the world contains both good and evil.

Examples of English writers of the Roman Noir include Mrs Ann Radcliffe (she was greatly imitated in France), Mary Shelley (*Frankenstein* (1818)), Wilkie Collins and Sheridan Le Fanu. French writers include Abbot Prévost, Vicomte d'Arlincourt (*Le Solitaire*), Victor Hugo (*Han d'Islande*) and Théophile Gautier (*La Morte Amoureuse*). American Gothic writers include Charles Brockden Brown, Nathaniel Hawthorne and Edgar Allan Poe.

In the 1930s, French publisher Gallimard had translated some of the emerging American writers including William Faulkner, James M Cain, Horace McCoy and Erskine Caldwell. They were very popular with readers, as well as with the leading French writers of the time. With the end of World War Two, Gallimard decided to launch a new imprint to publish the English and American Hard-Boiled novels they could not publish during the war. In August 1945, Série Noire was born under Marcel Duhamel's editorship. As well as meaning The Black Series the name was also a play on words because 'une série noire' literally means a succession of bad events. The first two titles were by Peter Cheyney, a British writer who emulated the American Hard-Boiled style. Cheyney and another Britisher, James Hadley Chase, had 12 titles between them in the first 30. The rest of the list was taken up by Raymond Chandler, Horace McCoy, W R Burnett, Dashiell Hammett and others. A success from the beginning because it mixed the successful Hard-Boiled with the gloomier 'maudit' (cursed, wretched) literature of Jim Thompson, David Goodis and others, each new title was assured of a first print run of 30,000 copies. The series became a staple of French literature and is soon to reach book number 2500.

Within the English language, the only use of Noir has been in Film Noir, to describe atmospheric crime films released from 1939 to 1958. (Film Noir was coined by French critic Nino Frank in 1946, but only came into common English usage in the early 1970s.)

Noir began to be used within crime fiction in 1983, when Nick Kimberley used 'noir' and 'maudit' to describe Jim Thompson's work in the introduction to the Black Box Thriller collection of 4 Jim Thompson novels. Then in 1984, Barry Gifford used the term Roman Noir in his introductions to the Black Lizard reprints of Jim Thompson's novels. Since then, Noir has been stuck onto the cover blurbs of many novels, although nobody seems to know what it means.

As a literary term, Noir can be applied to any work - especially one involving crime - that is notably dark, brooding, cynical, complex and pessimistic. This book is an attempt to list and explain these extended suicide notes. I will take you on a whistle-stop tour of some of these accursed writers. I will show you their anguish. I will give you a glimpse of some of the dark highways upon which they had to travel.

Dissection

> When thought is closed in caves
> Then love shall show its roots in deepest hell

> - William Blake

My sickness is called many things. Charles Willeford would call me an Immobilised Man, some French intellectuals would no doubt refer to my Existential angst, and yet others would refer to my Noir world-view.

Willeford's 1964 Masters Thesis about the Immobilised Man was published as *New Forms Of Ugly* (1987) in a limited edition of 350. His definition is: 'The immobilized hero, then, who is city-pent and agoraphobic, shares these characteristics: he 'writes' in the first person; he is antiscientific and antimaterialistic; he searches his own mind instead of going to the outside world for answers to his questions; he lives alone, counting and listing a small stock of possessions; he is a single man; he is likely to be an artist of sorts; his sense of humor is mordant, ironic, and often private; and he either loves or hates himself to the point of mental and physical pain.'

The immobilised man usually has his story told in the first person singular.

The immobilised man lives alone by choice. He usually lives in a single room, in a city.

The immobilised man is close to, but separated from, a vast number of people. Society dictates that you must interact with these people. The immobilised hero dreads coming into contact with them, and interacts with them as little as possible. He walks through the city, silently.

13

The immobilised man feels superior and is annoyed that other people fail to recognise his superiority.

The immobilised man feels free because only he knows the true nature of reality. He thinks himself aware, and everybody else asleep. They are ants, sheep, sleepwalkers.

The immobilised man thinks of himself as an artist (whether or not he is).

The immobilised man must survive somehow. He usually has a menial job (a penance to express his self-hate because he could do so much better) or he is an artist (singer, writer, painter, musician) and is quite happy to sponge off people he meets in bars.

The immobilised man tells us that he is looking for his true self, but he never really wants to face his true self - that would be too horrific. He would then have to acknowledge that he is like everybody else and, in that case, he would no longer be superior to them.

The immobilised man makes lists. He is trying to make sense of the world, so he approaches it empirically, listing all the things he has, or has done. Conversely, he lists all the things he has not done. This list is a way for him to make sense of a chaotic world. When he assesses his list, he usually finds that there is nothing of importance in his life, that he has nothing to show for existing, that he has done nothing to make the world a better place.

The immobilised man only carries on living because of his self-love. At some stage in the story, he tries to incorporate another human being into his world, so that they too can become aware of the horror of the world. This is his love object. When they do not fit, our hero expels them from his world, and he begins to doubt his self-love. It often becomes self-hate.

The immobilised man is not only immobilised by the confines of his room, he is also impotent in other areas. He cannot emotionally connect with other people, and he cannot sustain loving relationships with women.

After many months and years of muttering to himself about how horrible the world is, the immobilised man has to find a way to release all that pent-up anger and frustration. This act is usually murder - the ultimate taboo in our society. It is an act of self-hate because he wants to destroy the part of him that makes him like everybody else in society. This death wish results in either the immobilised man killing himself, or society killing him through public execution.

The immobilised man is one of the main forms of the Noir novel, and there are many variations on the theme. Fyodor Dostoyevsky's *Crime And Punishment* was in the third person instead of the first. Other novels, like Jim Thompson's *The Criminal*, have multiple points of view. Sometimes, the narrator may not be confined to a room but to a town, or street - a microcosm where they can explore their ideas. For example, William Lindsay Gresham's *Nightmare Alley* is set in the world of carnival freaks.

It should be noted that the author is not the immobilised man. The author constructs a text which often contains elements of his own life, to give it an authentic, autobiographical feel. Also, by talking directly to the reader, it gives a sense of intimacy. Although they often read like diaries, the Noir text is written for the reader to read. It is an artifice.

So why does the author write these Noir confessions? In many cases, the author is expressing their anger or outrage at the hypocrisy of the world. In *Prelude To A Certain Midnight*, Gerald Kersh points out that murderers are not always the only people to blame for murders - sometimes there are people who give the murderer the confidence to kill. Kersh's novel was published just after World War Two, when many people tried to shift any guilt away from themselves. Through his novels, Derek Raymond expresses his anger that the dead, the victims, are forgotten, so he constructs stories (*He Died With His Eyes Open*, *I Was Dora Suarez*) where the dead live once more to tell their tale. James Sallis has a more subtle agenda, with each novel making his way through a list of different types of pain, anguish and anxiety.

In Noir Fiction you have no control over your life, your future. The Great Maybe as Rabelais called it with his dying breath. Knowing this, you fall into a great despair. The French Existentialists were fans of Hard-Boiled and Noir literature. In Jean-Paul Sartre's *La Nausée/Nausea* (1938), and Albert Camus' *L'Etranger/The Outsider* (1942), they told us that anguish is at the core of human existence. We have been made to suffer. Camus said that this situation is absurd - we have been made so that we die (just like characters in books have been made to be killed). The immobilised man recognises this absurdity, and often makes fun of death and the meaninglessness of life. This is the root of his black humour.

History

The threads of Noir come from many different times and places around the world. It is a combination of the Gothic novel, the European naturalists, the German Expressionists, the American Hard-Boiled voice, the French Existentialists, Absurdists, Surrealists, the Proletarian writers of the 1930s. It is also a reaction to living in the cities after the Industrial Revolution, a reaction to living on top of each other but apart at the same time, and a reaction to increased leisure time allowing the masses too much time to think and develop paranoia, neuroses, schizophrenia. Noir Fiction is the literature of the modern age.

Fyodor Dostoyevsky: Joking With Clenched Teeth

Professor Milioukov said that, "A Russian lacks the cement of hypocrisy." What he meant was that society is held together by lies. For example: we are the centre of the universe; our life has meaning; we live on through our work/art/money/possessions/children; we are building for a future; we have a real and meaningful effect on the world. And Russians do not believe these lies. Certainly Fyodor Dostoyevsky did not.

It was Fyodor Dostoyevsky (1821-1881) who first got under the skin of his central characters and made us feel their intense pain, suffering and bewilderment. Initially a student of Gogol's work, Dostoyevsky found his own voice with *Notes From Underground* (1864) whose narrator is perhaps the earliest example of an immobilised man. In the first part, the central character tells us his thoughts about himself and the world he lives in. In the second part, he tells us the story of his relationship with a woman.

The novella begins, 'I am a sick man...I am an angry man. I am an unattractive man.' He lives in a room and talks about himself. He says he is well educated and that he is cleverer than everybody else. He plays tricks on people out of boredom because he is a lazy man. (He tells the reader that he is lying.) He believes that man's natural state is inertia, because thinking leads to uncertainty and self-doubt. Whereas, if you do things, you do not have time to think and life is therefore more certain. This sounds like a variation of Jean-Paul Sartre's definition of Existentialism - that man is defined by his actions.

The narrator makes the point that man continues to act barbarically despite becoming civilised. Man makes the excuse that he is acting according to his nature. Man is governed by his desires, his will, his volition. If he did not have these, he would be a mere object. And where is it written that man's desires must be normal and virtuous? In fact, man is naturally contrary and does not like to be told what to do. His will acts against his reason. History is certainly not the result of reason.

But what does man want to do with his will? Man loves to build, but he also loves to destroy. This is because he has an instinctive fear of attaining his goal. He is interested in the process of attaining his goal rather than the goal itself. So, the quest is the thing, not the grail. This is ridiculous - 'all this plainly amounts to a joke.' Which is why Dostoyevsky's narrator jokes with clenched teeth. His notion of the absurd - the word 'absurd' is used often throughout *Notes From Underground* - is similar to Albert Camus' in his Absurd novel *The Outsider*.

The narrator goes on to ask why people are so sure that what is normal and positive is good for man? Perhaps suffering is just as good for man as prosperity? Suffering, after all, is the sole cause of consciousness. 'Despair can hold the most intense sorts of pleasure when one is strongly conscious of the hopelessness of one's position.' Ultimately, 'we are born dead.'

Dostoyevsky was born October 30 1821 in the Moscow Hospital for the Poor where his father was Chief Medical Director. Although Dostoyevsky is often portrayed as a poor man of the people, his family were in fact from the professional class, and were trying to climb the financial and social ladder. As a boy, when his family was living at the Hospital, a close friend, a 9-year-old girl, was found raped in the courtyard - she died shortly afterwards. Dostoyevsky saw all the weak and crippled and downtrodden people whilst living there. He saw the suffering of life.

Dostoyevsky's father died on June 6 1839. For many years, it was believed that he was murdered by peasants wanting revenge, that the shock death began Dostoyevsky's epileptic fits, and that the residual psychological damage was the fuel for Dostoyevsky's novels, and the reason for Dostoyevsky's gambling, emotional and psychological problems. Sigmund Freud famously diagnosed Dostoyevsky in print based on these assumptions. They are all untrue.

According to Geir Kjetsaa's biography, the probable truth is that whilst travelling to a village to check on his late wife's land, Dr Dostoyevsky stopped to correct the work of some peasants. Whilst yelling at them, he collapsed in the intense heat, suffered an apoplectic attack and died through a lack of the appropriate medicine. Fyodor's reaction to his father's death, and lack of comment on it in later years, indicates that it did not have a tremendous bearing on his writing. Not unless it lies at the heart of his darkness, the darkness that cannot be described.

After the publication of *Poor Folk* (1846), the vain and self-centred Dostoyevsky, now living in St Petersburg, had difficulty in finding outlets for his writing. He frequented a club where he spoke and performed his work. After spontaneously spouting insurrection in the heat of the moment, he found himself, his brother Mikhail and 32 others, arrested on April 23 1849. They were imprisoned for 18 months then, on December 22, 22 of them were escorted to the public square and the waiting scaffold. Stripped to the waist, in a temperature of -21° F, it was at this moment that Dostoyevsky relayed to a fellow prisoner the idea for a book. Dressed in the long white shrouds of condemned men they were about to be shot when news came that the Tsar had commuted their sentences to hard labour in Siberia.

It was that moment of death, Dostoyevsky wrote, that was his salvation. He became intensely aware of every moment of life. He saw everything clearly for the first time. This was the true turning point of his life.

In the Siberian convict settlement, Dostoyevsky learnt everything he could about the psychology of his fellow inmates, whether they were murderers, thieves or political prisoners. In 1853, he was put into the army. In 1856, he returned to Siberia. Upon his release in 1859, Dostoyevsky worked as a journalist for 6 years. It was during this time that his epileptic attacks began - they were ecstatic experiences bringing him great joy, but leaving him weaker with each attack.

Dostoyevsky was one of 5 children, and he was closest to his brother Mikhail – they both had an interest in literary works, specifically Mrs Ann Radcliffe, Aleksander Pushkin, Walter Scott, Honoré de Balzac, Homer and Nikolai Gogol. With Mikhail as publisher and editor, and Dostoyevsky as main writer and creative driving force, they began *Time* magazine in September 1860. (Mikhail had sold his tobacco factory to finance it.) It featured Dostoyevsky's reminiscences of his time in Siberia, *The House Of The Dead*, which was a great success. However, the Tsar stopped *Time* in 1863 because of politically sensitive comments therein. Agreeing to be non-political, and a mouthpiece for the Tsar, the brothers were allowed to publish *Epoch*, beginning March 1864 - *Notes From Underground* appeared in the first 3 issues. Within 6 months, Mikhail, Maria (Dostoyevsky's sickly wife) and Dostoyevsky's best friend died. If *Notes From Underground* had been a psychological break with the joyful past, the deaths of those closest to him was a physical one.

To escape debtors from the collapse of *Epoch*, Dostoyevsky went abroad for 4 years, and had a miserable time. The Underground Man stopped writing and took action in Dostoyevsky's next project. *Crime And Punishment* (1866) is an extraordinary book which plunges the reader into the almost insane world-view of Raskolnikov, a young student who thinks himself superior to a grasping old woman who lends money. The woman is cruel and no good. She does not contribute to the world, so what does it matter if he kills her for her money and uses the money for good? So he kills her with an axe. Raskolnikov is compelled to kill despite his better reason. After the murder, which he gets away with, he tries to analyse why he did it. In the end, he feels guilty and gives himself up to the police.

It is one of the first books to look into the criminal mind, showing the hopes, fears and anger of the murderer in a series of frantic sequences. Philip Rahv summed it up in his article *Dostoyevsky In Crime And Punishment* (Partisan Review 27 (1960)), 'Never quite certain what it was exactly that induced him to commit murder, he must continually spy on himself in a desperate effort to penetrate his own psychology and attain the self-knowledge he needs if he is to assume responsibility for his absurd and hideous act.'

Whilst reading *Crime And Punishment*, you have the distinct impression that you are hearing Raskolnikov's thoughts throughout but surprisingly, it is written in the third person. In fact, Dostoyevsky had begun writing it from Raskolnikov's point of view but burnt the first draft because he did not think it appropriate. At the end, *Crime And Punishment* presents the reader with a solution which is not explained through logic; the criminal is cured through religion, much as Dostoyevsky himself became closer to God after his years in Siberia, but how Raskolnikov reached that decision is not shown. Perhaps the mysteriousness of religion is meant to symbolise the ultimate mystery of human nature...perhaps we will never be able to completely explain ourselves no matter how deeply we look.

Dostoyevsky went on to write *The Idiot* (1869) and *The Possessed/The Devils* (1872), then returned to St Petersburg in 1871 as a leading literary figure. In 1872, he began editing *The Citizen*, a weekly newspaper, where his *A Diary Of A Writer* (consisting of memoirs, notes and opinions) appeared as and when he completed them. He began work on *The Brothers Karamazov* in 1877, which remained unfinished when he died on January 28 1881.

Dostoyevsky has influenced generations of writers, from Rilke to Hermann Hesse, from Robert Louis Stevenson to Friedrich Nietzsche. In February 1887, Nietzsche read *Notes From Underground* and said that Dostoyevsky was "the only psychologist from whom he had anything to learn."

In a note which precedes *Notes From Underground*, Dostoyevsky writes, 'If we take into consideration the conditions that have shaped our society, people like the writer not only may, but must, exist in that society.' Noir Fiction is the biography of The Underground Man.

Joseph Conrad: We Live, As We Dream - Alone

Whereas *Crime And Punishment* tries to get inside the mind of Raskolnikov, *Heart Of Darkness* (1899) by Joseph Conrad (1857-1924) looks at the dark from the outside.

We begin on a yawl The Nellie, on the Thames River ('the very end of the world, a sea the colour of lead, a sky the colour of smoke'), where 5 men wait for the tide to change. The narrator tells us that one of the men, Marlow, recounts a story while they wait. He is a seaman, the only one of the 5 who still follows the sea. He describes a symbolic journey into the dense Congo jungles on behalf of The Company - he is to learn and take over a river route. Once there, he hears rumours of Kurtz, an employee of The Company who has gone out of control - the natives revere him as a God. The story follows Marlow's journey as he gets closer and closer to the mysterious Kurtz.

Although plotted as a rite of passage for Marlow, it soon becomes apparent that Marlow will never learn about the darkness because he is blind to its meaning. He knows it is there, and he can see its effect on the people around him, but he cannot define or understand it. Consequently, he cannot connect the darkness in the jungles with the darkness that lies outside them, in the people and the places that he thinks constitute a civilised world. Yet, Conrad links the Thames and the Congo, as one long river, saying that just as all the seas and rivers are interconnected, so is mankind.

Kurtz is a symbol of men who are 'hollow at the core,' who succumb to their unconscious desires once placed outside the influence of civilised society. Without those outer restraints, they are helpless because they have no inner restraint. Conrad illustrates this by comparing the hungry cannibals on the boat (who show restraint by not eating the passengers!) with the heads on poles in front of Kurtz' house which 'showed that Mr Kurtz lacked restraint in the gratification of his various lusts.'

Conrad is also comparing the societies. On his way to the Congo, Marlow stops at a city which reminds him of a white sepulchre. In biblical terms a white sepulchre represented a hypocrite whose light/white/outward righteousness and pleasantness concealed inner corruption. This then is the theme - the white colonials in darkest Africa are revealed as hypocritical corrupters of the natives. Conrad refers to a time when the whites were once natives themselves, implying that civilisation has corrupted the soul, and further implying that only nature is pure and sublime.

In a letter to a friend, written just after he completed *Heart Of Darkness*, Conrad wrote, 'Man is a vicious animal...Crime is a necessary condition of an organised existence. Society is essentially criminal.'

Józef Teodor Konrad Korzeniowki (he shortened his name because he could not bear to hear people mispronounce it) was born into Polish aristocracy on December 3 1857. In Warsaw in 1861, his father was arrested for conspiracy against his Russian rulers. The family was exiled to Volgoda in Russia, where they suffered from the harsh climate. By the time he was 11, both of Conrad's parents were dead and he was put into the care of his uncle.

Aged 16, Conrad journeyed to France to begin a seafaring life. For 4 years he tried, and although the sailors of Marseilles respected his work (they knew him by name and called upon him to guide boats safely to harbour), Conrad could not obtain the necessary permits to sail with a ship. In an effort to earn a living, he turned to gun-smuggling, and then lost all his money on his first attempt at roulette. In despair - without money and employment (and perhaps losing a love, as implied in his short story *The Arrow Of Gold* (1918)) - Conrad shot himself, the bullet passing through his body, just missing the heart and other vital organs.

After recovering, Conrad went to England where he became the first Pole to become a Master in the British Merchant Service. He had many adventures, shipwrecks, hardships and after 15 years at sea began writing a novel (*Almayer's Folly* (1895)) while resting in London.

When Henry Morton Stanley opened up the Congo and publicised its riches in his books, the Congo was soon overrun by fortune hunters who ripped out its heart. In 1890, Conrad went to the Congo, a place he had wanted to explore from childhood and part of the motivation for his desire to become an able seaman. Events occurred almost exactly as described in *Heart Of Darkness*. He went on a trip to learn his route, and had to take command when the captain became ill - their objective was to collect the Company's agent Georges Antoine Klein, who died on the way back. (Kurtz was first called Klein until Conrad changed it.) Conrad also met Hodister, a successful explorer and Company agent who was a member of the 'gang of virtue,' which condemned slavery and barbaric customs. Conrad used Hodister for elements of Kurtz. Generally, it was a vile place full of the worst kinds of people. Matters were not helped when he clashed with the Company's acting director Camille Delcommune, who hated the English, and considered Conrad one. Conrad's boat was under repair, and would not be ready for months. In the meantime, Delcommune prevented Conrad from doing useful work or going on expeditions. After 4 months, sick with fever and dysentery (his health was never the same), Conrad left. The Congo laid bare for Conrad the vast difference between what men say (pretensions) and what men do (practice). This hypocrisy lies at the heart of Conrad's writing. His reaction to the human baseness he witnessed ranged from black humour in *An Outpost Of Progress* (1897) to horror in *Heart Of Darkness*.

Eventually returning to England, Conrad finished *Almayer's Folly* and became an author of repute, mixing with Henry James, HG Wells, Stephen Crane and other prominent literary figures of the day. *Heart Of Darkness* was begun in December 1898 and completed in the first week of February. Conrad said that it was very near the truth of his expedition into the Congo. It was first published in the February-April 1899 issues of *Blackwood's Magazine*. Conrad took Marlow and his companions (the Director of Companies, The Lawyer, The Accountant, and the narrator) from *Youth* (1902), and he would reuse them again in *Lord Jim* (1899) and *Chance* (1912).

The journey down the river is a journey through the dark highways of the mind. Albert J Guérard called it a 'night journey.' Others may call it a dark night of the soul. It combines elements of the quest, where the hero is transformed by undergoing a rite of passage. The journey is marked by the Company Station, then Central Station and finally the Inner Station. Not only are we going inside, we are going back in time, stripping the veneer of civilisation to find out what people are made of.

If you consider that we are born with instinct (what we all have in common: survival; hunting; foraging; community) and nature (our individual motivations), and that experience is something we acquire after birth, then at the Inner Station we find out our true nature. At his death Kurtz cries out, "The horror! The horror!" On the cusp of extinction, Kurtz gains self-knowledge, an emotional understanding of his experience. He has one piercing moment of clarity. Life, according to Marlow, is 'that mysterious arrangement of merciless logic for a futile purpose.'

The style of Conrad's writing is both direct and obscure. Direct in that he describes the external workings of things for us to discern the inner truth, like the Existentialists would later claim actions define a person. He is obscure because Conrad's words become more vague and inconclusive as we approach the darkness. Certainly, if we could describe and understand the darkness then we could identify it. Then it would no longer be unknown and dark.

Marlow fails to understand the darkness. This is because the darkness must remain an unsettling presence, always hovering on the periphery of our understanding, troubling our consciousness. We live in times when everything is analysed, explained and defined. We are taught that if you find the centre then you will find meaning. *Heart Of Darkness* denies this. At the end, Marlow does not solve any mysteries. He is not transformed, like in normal quest stories. There is no answer, only dread of the 'immense darkness.'

Conrad went on to write many fine stories and novels including *Nostromo* (1904), *The Secret Agent* (1907), *Under Western Eyes* (1911) before passing away in 1924, but it is *Heart Of Darkness* and its themes that continue to influence and inspire others including George Orwell's *Nineteen Eighty-Four* (1948), William Golding's *Lord Of The Flies* (1954), Louis-Ferdinand Céline's *Journey To The End Of The Night* (1932) and the work of T S Eliot, whose *The Hollow Men* refers to Kurtz who is 'hollow at the core.' (The autobiographical central character of Norwegian Knut Hamsun's *Hunger* (1890) wanders the streets of Christiania (now Oslo) starving. His hunger is a metaphor for the absence of spiritual nourishment within. He tells us 'I seemed to myself hollowed out from head to toe,' and echoes further Noir tendencies when he later says 'I lay with eyes open in a sense of alienation from myself. I felt wonderfully out of myself,' and even later that 'The dark had captured my brain and gave me not an instant of peace. What if I myself become dissolved into the dark, turned into it?')

So it seems that not only is the immobilised man an underground man, he is a hollow man as well. The hollow man who represents the spiritual emptiness at the centre of existence.

Interiors

Significantly, *Crime & Punishment* and *Heart Of Darkness* predate the rise of psychology in 1900, when Sigmund Freud's *Interpretation Of Dreams* first appeared. The psychoanalysts tried to apply cold logic to the illogical subconscious which, at that time, was experiencing a massive upheaval from the Industrial Revolution.

The Industrial Revolution, fuelled by the love for money, planned for the masses and was not concerned with the idiosyncrasies and uniqueness of the individual. As the populace migrated to the cities to stoke the machines of the Industrial Revolution, they became lost within giant structures they could not control. After the relative freedom of the countryside, being trapped in the confines of rotting, disease-infested buildings, was traumatic for many.

The Expressionists were a disparate group of artists who used their paintings to assault the emotions before the brain had time to think. They tried to communicate the state of mind of the individual within his environment using the ground-breaking methods and styles of the Impressionists. The Impressionists showed the colours of nature and rural buildings, and were great experimenters, but they ignored the most important element of all - man. The Expressionists put man in urban, industrial surroundings, talked about sexual and social politics, and didn't hold their feelings back. The violence of their technique and the force of their arguments, gave the viewer no other option than to react, to express his own opinion on the matter. The reaction was often shock, followed by censorship and, occasionally, prison for the artists. Society couldn't approach the answers to the questions the Expressionists raised with any degree of honesty. The hypocrisy of the age, then as now, dictated that everyone was entitled to their own opinion as long as they didn't express it to anyone else.

The protagonists of the Expressionist movement were centred in Europe. In *The Scream* (1893), Norway's Edvard Munch (1863-1944) showed how the environment expressed the inner anguish of the central character. Viennese artist, Egon Schiele (1890-1918), painted explicit sexual situations where strong and weak people lost themselves in their own sexuality. Schiele saw these characters as being apart from the world, so he painted them in a void, with little or no background. Schiele's contemporary, Oscar Kokoschka (1886-1980), found his most potent images in portraits. Previously, portraits had been idealised in order to present the sitter in the best light, but the Expressionists looked behind the visage to put the sitter's inner nature on the canvas. This furthered the contemporary myth that artists, in whichever field, have some kind of insight that others do not. This is plainly untrue - they just talk about it more openly and use their art to express it.

In most cases, Expressionism dealt with the common man and his relationship to his oppressive environment. Since the environment was basically determined by the rich and powerful, who were exploiting the workers for gain, it was easy to see who the Expressionists targeted. The early part of this century was a time of volatile politics and artists like George Grosz (1893-1959) commented on the social conditions to make political statements.

Franz Kafka (1883-1924) took the Expressionists' reflection of society one step further by making bureaucracy and hypocrisy of society the Noir part of his novels. *The Trial* (1925) is about K, who is arrested and interrogated about a crime he is accused of committing. Trapped in the surreal world of bureaucracy, K tries to combat something he can't see or touch. In the end, K is assassinated without knowing the crime of which he was accused. The Noir cannot be stopped or altered - the Noir will always continue. You can only try to live with it.

Depression (1931-1939)

Although many writers have no other purpose than to entertain you, to divert your attention for a few hours as they spin a story, there are some who use the form for different reasons. These are critical writers, people not happy with the world and the way it is. Many writers took up the cause of the common people, the proletariat, the masses.

One of the most interesting English writers of the 1930s, now all but forgotten, is James Curtis. Whilst Edgar Wallace, Peter Cheyney and James Hadley Chase followed the American slanguage into the Hard-Boiled school, and Graham Greene examined the effects of sin, damnation and redemption in *The Man Within* (1929) and *Brighton Rock* (1938), Curtis used the language of the British streets and slums (like American writers Theodore Dreiser and Upton Sinclair) to comment on social conditions. He wrote about people in the hard parts of London, where it was accepted that you resorted to crime to survive. They had no other way out of their lives. They were confronted with situations, reacted to them, and were then confronted with even more problems. His characters did not have time to reflect on their lives, and only just enough time to live them. His novels (*The Gilt Kid* (1936), *You're In The Racket Too* (1937), *There Ain't No Justice* (1937), *They Drive By Night* (1938), *What Immortal Hand* (1939) and *Look Long Upon A Monkey*

(1956)) are books about victims, about people who will never ever succeed because the whole world is against them. They are not romantic or sentimental. There are no easy endings. There certainly is no justice that Curtis' books remain out of print and forgotten.

In America, the Depression hit bad. The people felt it hard. Authors like John Dos Passos, Daniel Fuchs and Dalton Trumbo generally portrayed the daily grind of the proletariat on the East coast of America, whilst B Traven picked more exotic settings. Some authors wrote novels as propaganda, holding up the common man as some kind of paragon of virtue. However, writers, like P J Wolfson, Nathanael West, James M Cain and Horace McCoy told the story of the West coast, where dreams were crushed on a daily basis, and the dreamers probably deserved to be crushed as well.

PJ Wolfson: Jazz And Tears And Death

The odds are that the name P J Wolfson means absolutely nothing to you. He is virtually unknown to readers in his native America, or in the UK. Even those who know a lot about Noir and Hard-Boiled fiction will more often than not give a blank look upon the mention of his name. Yet, in France, he is highly regarded by many crime writers who know of his one great novel: *Bodies Are Dust*.

Pincus Jacob Wolfson was born on May 22 1903 and died in Calabasas, Los Angeles, in April 1979. Very little is known about what happened in between. After the publication of his first novel *Bodies Are Dust* in 1931, Wolfson was summoned by Hollywood and he lost no time establishing a career there. He wrote almost 30 movies in 10 years, most of them in collaboration and some based on his stories. Some had great titles like *70,000 Witnesses* (1932), *The Devil Is Driving* (1932), *Night World* (1932) and *Reckless* (1935). Perhaps the most intriguing title is *Boy Slaves* (1939), the only film Wolfson wrote, produced and directed. About half of his scripts were crime thrillers and the rest were romantic comedies. This combination of the anti-social villain and the domestic situation is also the mixture most prevalent in his novels.

As well as his film career, Wolfson continued as a writer, publishing *Summer Hotel* (1932), *All Women Die* (1933, also as *Three Of A Kind* (1957) and as *This Woman Is Mine* (1959)), and *Is My Flesh Of Brass?* (1934 also as *Pay For Her Passion* (1949, abridged) and as *The Flesh Baron* (1954)). *All Women Die* is about a man who loses the only woman he ever loved and, over the years, is unable to forget her. Then she turns up, married to his brother. *Is My Flesh Of Brass?* is about two surgeons who perform illegal operations on the women they love. This is a hospital drama with the melodramatic twists you would expect of such a subject.

However, Wolfson's most devastating use of domestic melodrama was in *Bodies Are Dust* (1931 and as *Hell Cop* (1960)). In 1933, *Bodies Are Dust* was translated into French by Marcel Duhamel as *Corps perdu*, although it is now known as *A nos amours!* It has been reprinted several times in France, the last time in 1993, but has remained out of print in America for 40 years.

Bodies Are Dust is about Inspector Safiotte who is annoyed that he was passed over for Commissioner. By his admission, 'The top was always my end, and I trampled everything under foot for that.' Still, as an Inspector, he makes plenty of money from the speakeasies, whores, gambling dens and dope peddlers, and 'could have the choice of the nicest women.' Then, he gets a horrendous pain in his stomach - he feels better when he vomits so he puts off going to the doctor.

Safiotte has very definite ideas. He tells his housekeeper, who has an illegitimate child, that he cannot understand why she does not give the child away to a home. He does not like children. He has sex with many women, whenever he wants and with whomever he wants. Unlike his bodyguard and best friend, The Arm, he does not believe that sex with one woman could remain interesting over many years. "I never wanted a woman so bad that I had to marry her to get it," Safiotte says. He hates hospitals and religion - so he dislikes Father Frank Laughlin who is a Professor of anatomy. "You cut up bodies?" Safiotte asks. "Yes." "Women's bodies?" "And children's too," the priest says.

As the story unfolds, several strands begin to emerge. First, there is his honest childhood friend Teeny (Tinevelli) who owns a respectable bank which was 'like a clean spot on a sore skin.' Teeny offers to return Safiotte's dirty money and it later emerges that Teeny stole money from the bank to pay a blackmailing gang. Also, through his drug dealer contacts, Safiotte learns that the upcoming big fight is fixed and that counterfeit tickets are on sale - Safiotte cuts himself in on 10% of the money from the counterfeit tickets. All the time, he is sore that the Mayor passed him over for Commissioner - the Mayor promises that the current Commissioner will not be there for long.

Safiotte is distracted by other events. His appendix explodes and he has to have an emergency operation - perversely, he asks for his head to be raised so that he can see himself be cut open. Recovering in hospital, he makes love to a nurse who has a weak heart. Since her husband died, she cannot stop making love - she dies. Then he falls in love with Beth, The Arm's new wife. Safiotte remembers his young love for Nina. She left, but he ran into her again when he raided a call-house - his ability to love died, but is been rekindled by Beth.

The scene having been set, the rest of the story is about how Safiotte gets Beth. When Teeny goes missing, Safiotte assigns The Arm to guard duty at Teeny's house, allowing Safiotte to visit Beth. They talk. He asks her if she ever wanted to do a terrible thing because "Nothing is terrible to me...What we do, well, we do because it is in us...born with you...I can't stop myself from doing some things." "Then you're putting your appetite, your stomach, where your head should be. Your mind should control your body," she tells him. "That's right. My mind thinks and my body follows it up." "Then you don't think right."

There is a manhunt for Teeny but Safiotte does not care - he can only think of Beth. He visits her, tells her that he loves her and finds out she is equally smitten. They make love, and plan to meet again. All the time, Safiotte wonders how long it will take before his love for her becomes cold and hard. Later, they fight and Beth decides that they should break up, even though she loves him, because she feels like a whore. Safiotte says he loves her, that he'll marry her if she divorces, but their affair is over.

When Teeny's body is found - he committed suicide - Safiotte tracks down the blackmailer, shoots him and claims self-defence.

Talking to MacDunn about love, Safiotte says: "It's wonderful and sometimes when you can't get it the way you want, it's like something trying to tear your guts out." Safiotte gets drunk, and goes with a girl, but he can only think of Beth with The Arm. Soon, Safiotte hates The Arm. He goes for a walk and decides that it does not matter whether The Arm lives a few more days or a few less. Safiotte gets his druggie friend to think he is wanted, then sends The Arm to get him - The Arm is shot dead. Four weeks after the funeral, Safiotte visits Beth to see how she is. She tells him she is pregnant and the child is his. He does not care for the child, but says he loves her and wants to marry her. They marry a week later.

Safiotte lives to the rhythm of domestic life and Beth gives birth to a baby girl. Time passes. 'I found the child in my mind all the time,' Safiotte thinks. When he returns home one night, he finds that the baby has vomited so he cleans her up and gives her some water. She vomits that up also, so they give her an enema and all the poison comes out. They sleep.

Safiotte goes into work the following morning. "I'm not hating anything so much," he tells MacDunn, who says that Safiotte is getting old and soft. "Soft - what's soft? I guess it's satisfaction. No more little devils pushing pins into your backside, making you get up and walk around and do and do. Drink and do and fight and crush until you fall down and can't feel the pins anymore. Soft - a wall that keeps the devils out."

The baby is still sick, so the doctor and a baby specialist are called out. Safiotte desperately gets the prescription, orders the nurses and delivers a sample to the laboratory. The results say that the baby has a cerebral inflammation. Safiotte goes out into the rain and just wants to drink and drown and die. The baby dies that night. Safiotte and Beth mourn. Safiotte prays to God - a God he said he did not believe in.

And the papers announce that the Police Commissioner has just resigned.

This is an extraordinary book. Not just because of its hard-edged prose, or its frank attitude towards sex, but because it shows the internal workings of a bad man. There are no clichés or undue melodrama, only a direct connection between him and us. The *New York Herald Tribune* called *Bodies Are Dust*, 'The most exciting as well as the most brutal of all the many contemporary tales with New York underworld, police and political backgrounds.' The *New York Times* said that it had, 'power...ruthless tempo...sense of elemental emotions controlling man's destiny.'

This is the crux of the story. Safiotte is going up in the world by making things happen (graft, murder, corruption, blackmail), but all the events that cause him the most trouble are outside his control (appendix, falling in love, the baby dying). This is a fight between human nature, the environment he lives in, and destiny/fate/God.

After working in films up to the 1950s, Wolfson wrote another novel *How Sharp The Point* (1959 and translated into French as *Bataille de coqs* (1968)) and went on to write 150 television shows before drifting into obscurity.

Nathanael West: What Is The Whole Stinkin Business For?

W H Auden called it 'West's Disease.' Whilst most writers concentrated on the material poverty of the world in the 1930s, Nathanael West wrote incessantly and passionately about the spiritual poverty which infested all areas of society.

Utter the words 'Hollywood,' '1930s,' and 'Novelists' and you can come up with a long list of famous writers, taking the dirty money, spending it on booze, despairing that they were churning out entertainment instead of art. Some authors, however, were invigorated by the atmosphere and produced great novels. Such as Nathanael West. He wrote the surreal *The Dream Life Of Balso Snell* (1931), the manic *Miss Lonelyhearts* (1933), the depressing *A Cool Million* (1934) and the desperate *The Day Of The Locust* (1939). His work for Hollywood began in July 1933 (on *Beauty Parlour*), but he had to wait until 1936 before his first script was produced (*Ticket To Paradise*). He gained a string of solo screen credits before being elevated to 'polisher' - a respected position where he would take an existing script and spend 2 weeks or so improving the work of others just before filming began. Where F Scott Fitzgerald tied himself in knots trying to write art for film (and being rewritten by hacks), West thought the whole situation absurd because he knew the end result would turn out to be meaningless. It is this element of the absurd which is ever present in his novels, and probably best shown in his second novel.

Miss Lonelyhearts (1933) begins as a joke and gradually transforms into a catastrophe. The joke is this: The *New York Post-Dispatch* hit upon the wheeze of employing a male Miss Lonelyhearts for their agony aunt. Miss Lonelyhearts takes the joke, and then finds it sticks in his throat. Reading letters from Sick-of-it-all (she has had 7 children in 12 years, is ill, and a Catholic), Desperate (she is a girl with no nose who wants a boyfriend), and Harold S (he is trying to stop his little sister from being abused), Miss Lonelyhearts feels sick and takes to brooding. His editor Shrike (a reference to Munch's *The Scream/Shriek*?) is totally unmoved by Miss Lonelyhearts' compassion/guilt. Miss Lonelyhearts visits Betty, the woman he loves, but he is too violent/disturbed and she asks him to leave.

Finding his friends, they amuse themselves by telling stories of gang-bangs and rape. Once they believed in literature and the 'beauty' which it could contain, but no longer. One of them says, "The trouble with him, the trouble with all of us, is that we have no outer life, only an inner one, and that by necessity." And further, "He wants to cultivate his interior garden." This is a reference to Voltaire's *Candide* (1759), a quest novel wherein the central character travels the world and finds it repulsive. Recoiling from the world, Candide decides to look after his own garden (i.e. improve himself), in the (perhaps vain) hope that others will follow his example.

Rejected by his love, but still desperate for sex, Miss Lonelyhearts tries Mrs Shrike but, after wining and dining her and lathering her up, she does the deed with her husband (who is too mean to pay for the wining and dining, and too lazy to do the lathering). Even more desperate, Miss Lonelyhearts beds Fay, a fan.

Miss Lonelyhearts falls sick with despair. He explains to Betty that the letters, 'are profoundly humble pleas for moral and spiritual advice, that they are inarticulate expressions of genuine suffering.' For the first time in his life he is being taken seriously and he is forced to examine the values by which he lives. Betty thinks that all his troubles are city troubles, so they spend a love-filled idyll in the country.

As soon as he returns to the city Miss Lonelyhearts knows he is not cured because he cannot forget the letters (the horror, cruelty, absurdity of the world). He makes the observation that men always fight their misery with dreams, but dreams have lost their power, 'they have been made puerile by the movies, radio and newspapers.' (And television presumably.)

Miss Lonelyhearts transforms. He becomes humble when he reads the heart-breaking story of Broad-Shoulders. He becomes apart from the world seeing as if he were an outsider. A cripple, Peter Doyle, hands him a letter into which he has poured his whole heart. Doyle asks Miss Lonelyhearts, 'What is the whole stinkin business for?' What is the point of life? Why does he go through the pain and suffering, walking up and down stairs with his bad leg to feed/support his family? He thought Miss Lonelyhearts might know since he is a man of education. Miss Lonelyhearts is now a priest-like figure. They hold hands under the table. It is a tender moment. (Earlier, Shrike, in a rare moment of reflection, said, "I adore heart-to-heart talks and nowadays there are so few people with whom one can really talk. Everybody is so hard-boiled.... It is better to make a clean breast of matters than to let them fester in the depths of one's soul.") Miss Lonelyhearts is a magnet for lonely hearts and feels the need to take their suffering upon himself. He is becoming a martyr. He feels their pain.

Invited to dinner at the Doyles', the night is a complete disaster - Doyle's wife Fay is the fan Miss Lonelyhearts slept with. Fay and Peter argue all the time. Fay is the dominant one. She humiliates Peter. When Peter goes out for cigarettes, Fay comes on to Miss Lonelyhearts. Disgusted, Miss Lonelyhearts hits Fay repeatedly and leaves.

Miss Lonelyhearts is so sensitive to the pain of the world that he cannot allow any of it to get past his defences. He becomes more aloof/retreats from the world. He is impenetrable, a rock, and a rock does not care for the sea of troubles around it. 'Shrike dashed against him, but fell back, as a wave that dashes against an ancient rock, smooth with experience, falls back.' Betty announces she is pregnant and Miss Lonelyhearts (the rock) can handle it. They agree to marry and plan their future together. 'He did not feel guilty. He did not feel.' Miss Lonelyhearts felt he had a religious conversion. He was full of God, whole again. (Developing a Christ-like demeanour, he remembers words from Dostoyevsky's *The Brothers Karamazov*, 'Love a man even in his sin.') Doyle turns up (he thinks Miss Lonelyhearts tried to rape Fay). Miss Lonelyhearts goes to embrace him in love. Doyle hobbles down the stairs. Betty enters. Doyle shoots Miss Lonelyhearts, and together they fall down the stairs, towards Betty.

Comic, grotesque, surreal, horrific. And true. *Miss Lonelyhearts* began one night in March 1929 when a columnist who wrote an agony aunt column under the name Susan Chester, showed West and his friend S J Perelman some of the letters she received, pointing out how funny they were. West did not see them that way. The pathos of the one signed Broad-Shoulders haunted West and he decided he had to write something about these people. West finished the book in December 1932, including the (heavily revised) letters as part of the text.

Miss Lonelyhearts is an immobilised man. He lives in a room, lists the contents (bed, table, 2 chairs), feels sick with the world, is obsessed by order but everything becomes chaos, reads a lot of books, thinks himself superior to the people crying out for help. But, no matter how witty he is, he cannot escape the fact that the pain the people feel is the same as the pain he feels inside himself. At the beginning, Miss Lonelyhearts writes, in reply to a letter, 'Life *is* worthwhile.' He believes this, but it sounds trite. Later, when he tries to reconcile Peter and Fay Doyle at the disastrous dinner night, Miss Lonelyhearts spouts one cliché after another. His religious conversion echoes Raskolnikov's in *Crime And Punishment*. His lack of eloquence echoes

Kurtz' in *Heart Of Darkness*. Miss Lonelyheart's speechlessness is ironic, since he makes his living from words. Yet, from the beginning, he cannot write. But his creator has no problem finding the right words. For example, when Shrike kisses one of his women, West writes, 'he buried his triangular face like the blade of a hatchet, into her neck.'

Dreams play an important part in the novel - Miss Lonelyhearts dreams constantly. West says that the press and radio are trivialising man's dreams, that dreams have lost their power. Here is a novel which is one long, powerful dream. Although Miss Lonelyhearts is still optimistic enough to dream, the other characters seem to have given up their dreams. They have no dreams to help them deal with their misery. Miss Lonelyhearts found his dream - his dream of Christ.

Published on April 8 1933, Miss Lonelyhearts received some great reviews from his friends, but most concluded that it was too vile, ugly, distasteful, depressing to sell many copies. Ironically, West and his publisher received (anonymous) phone calls from people from all over America threatening to sue him, claiming that he had reprinted their letters without their permission. He struck a chord - loneliness and alienation were good subjects for the 1930s. Just as all the reviews were coming in, and demand for the book was rising, the publisher decided to declare himself bankrupt, to clear his debts. As a result, the printers held back 2,000 copies of the 2,200 print run. Also, the stock market crashed. In May, West managed to get a reprint deal with another publisher. Also, a film reader thought *Miss Lonelyhearts* was a great book and advised West to submit a synopsis. It became the dire comedy *Advice To The Lovelorn* (1933) but it got West into Hollywood and onto the first rung of the ladder of success.

One of West's books, a biography of Vincent Van Gogh, has a section ruled in it which reads, '...instead of giving myself up to passive melancholy, I have chosen active despair...' West may have written about despair, but he was not the kind of person to indulge in it himself. In the end, he did not have time to think about it. Just as both his Hollywood and literary careers were taking off, Nathanael West and his wife died in a car accident on December 22 1940.

'I...can scarcely believe that life could be so cruel to me,' writes one of the lonely hearts. Believe it. Life can be cruel, no matter how hard you try to deny it.

James M Cain: She Knew What To Do

Both Hammett and Chandler liked to write about people with money and power, and the way that they abused it. There is always the feeling of other-worldliness, of hyper-reality, when reading their polished words. Also, the private dick was never going to die or get maimed for the rest of the series, no matter how many times he got hit over the head, thrown off a cliff, or shot at in a locked room. There was no change in the central character so the 'danger' of damage to the reader's sensibilities was limited.

However, there were writers whose main protagonists were liable to potential change. The most well-known in the 1930s was probably James M Cain (1892-1977) who took the taboos and emotions of ordinary people and added a twist of fate to ensure they got their come-uppance. Cain littered his stories with strong men and women whose compulsive love is hindered by one stumbling block after another. Eventually, the lovers must resort to crime and, in doing so, condemn themselves to a life apart. Cain's work was often defeatist, because whatever his characters fought for was ultimately lost - either through their own doing, or by the mysterious hand of fate. The dream was never fulfilled.

Cain began writing his first novel in February 1933, combining ideas that had been in his head. He remembered a girl at a gas station who had apparently killed her husband. With screenwriter Vincent Lawrence (to whom he dedicated the novel), he discussed the 1927 Ruth Snyder-Judd Gray murder case, where the lovers killed Albert Snyder, and then Ruth tried to kill off Judd afterwards.

The story begins with homeless Frank Chambers walking into a remote gas station/lunchroom in the San Fernando Valley, where he takes a job working for owner Nick Papadakis when he sees the wife, Cora. It turns out that Cora is a woman of the world, who was stuck in a joint and was happy to get out when Nick proposed to her. Now Cora is unhappy. That is, until Frank comes into her life. They begin a passionate affair and it becomes apparent that they have to kill Nick. After fouling up their first attempt, they succeed in throwing him over a steep embankment. Cora is accused of murder and stands trial.

Cain wrote 80,000 words of lawyers throwing words at each other which was boring, so he did a bit of research. Talking to Mr Harrington of the AAA insurance division, Cain asked if it was possible for two insurance companies to pay off a third if Cora was found guilty, because they would lose less money that way. Possible? It had happened to Harrington! Cain cut the 80,000 words.

Cain cut more words. He was fed up with writing 'he said' and 'he says' all over the manuscript, so he simply dropped them, leaving it up to the reader's intelligence to work out who was saying what. This stylistic device became Cain's trademark.

Having got away with the crime, Frank and Cora settle down to a life of boring domesticity. Cora turns the lunchroom into a thriving business. Frank paces around the place like a caged tiger. (Cats are very important to the story, turning up throughout the narrative, seeming to symbolise the unpredictability of life/events and the instinctive nature of man.) Frank has a romantic fling whilst Cora is away, and then they both fight for their lives when blackmailers come calling. Finally, Cora is pregnant and there is bliss between the couple. Cora dies. Frank, who is blameless, is tried and found guilty. The novel then, is told from his point of view, telling his confession from his jail cell, to a priest. Frank Chambers echoes contemporary characters Robert Syverten (*They Shoot Horses, Don't They?*) and Meursault (*The Outsider*). In her article in *Tough Guy Writers Of The Thirties*, Joyce Carol Oates also compares Frank to Julien Sorel from Stendhal's *The Red And The Black* (1830).

Originally titled *Bar-B-Que* when he finished it in June 1933, this 35,000 word novel was considered too short by his publisher Alfred Knopf who passed on it. Luckily, Knopf's wife liked it, so a deal was made. Cain thought of alternative titles (*Black Puma*, *The Devil's Checkbook*) before settling on *The Postman Always Rings Twice*. It went on to sell millions of copies.

James M Cain was born July 1 1892, and trained for the opera until he was told he would never make it. He retained a lifelong love of opera, which may explain the heightened melodrama of his plots. (*Serenade* (1937) is about a failed opera singer in Mexico.) After serving in World War One as editor of an army newspaper, Cain pursued a career in journalism, becoming a respected editorial man of the *New York World*. He was very close friends with H L Mencken whilst at the *American Mercury* and his pieces for the magazine were collected into Cain's first book, *Our Government* (1930). (Mencken went on to publish *Black Mask* magazine to generate the money to fund an ailing *American Mercury*.) Whilst working for *The New Yorker*, Cain got an offer of work from Hollywood which he grabbed with both hands. From 1932 to 1947, Cain worked on many scripts but only had 3 screen credits, the most famous being for *Algiers* (1938). With the publication of *The Postman*

Always Rings Twice punching him into the limelight, this and subsequent novels and stories had no problem being adapted for the screen during the 1940s.

Cain's novels mostly revolved around a woman getting a man to do her bidding. She is the femme fatale. *Double Indemnity* (1943), the classic story of a woman getting a man to kill her husband to get the insurance money, was written when work for the studios dried up. Cain sold it to *Liberty* magazine in 1936 as a serial, where it reportedly added 8 million to *Liberty*'s circulation. *Mildred Pierce* (1941) is the story of a woman who uses men for her own ends, gains money and power, then loses it all. *The Butterfly* (1947) is a novel of incest and revenge in the backwoods of the deep South.

When *The Moth* (1948) failed, Cain left Hollywood to do some serious writing. He continued writing good books, like *The Magician's Wife* (1965) and *Rainbow's End* (1975), but public interest had waned. His time had passed. And then he passed away on October 27 1977.

Cain's theme remained throughout his writing career: if your deepest, darkest wish comes true, you will pay a heavy, perhaps the ultimate price.

In his introduction to *The Butterfly*, Cain wrote, 'I belong to no school, hard-boiled or otherwise, and I believe these so-called schools exist mainly in the imagination of critics, and have little correspondence in reality anywhere else.' He would probably have disliked his work being categorised as Noir Fiction, but the fact remains that his books are peopled by the cursed, and we see/feel their anguish.

Horace McCoy: I'm Tired Of Living And I'm Afraid Of Dying

On one level Hammett and Chandler were successful with the public because they had morally correct endings. The villains died or went to jail (where they were executed), and the heroes tut-tutted. But the real Noir writers, the writers who put unpredictable people in unpredictable situations were writers like Horace McCoy (1897-1955). He created emotional and physical tension by forcing the reader to get involved with largely unsympathetic people who had been beaten by the world and didn't have the will to fight back. His characters are drawn into, and then consumed by, the abyss.

In *The Myth Of Sisyphus* (1942), Albert Camus wrote, 'There is but one serious philosophical problem, and that is suicide.' Bearing this in mind, it is no wonder that he and the existentialists seized upon McCoy's debut novel *They Shoot Horses, Don't They?* (1935) and labelled it the first American existentialist novel - it is one long suicide note.

They Shoot Horses, Don't They? is surrounded by death. Between each chapter are the words read out in court as the death sentence on Robert Syverten is passed. The novel, then, is his reminiscence of what happened. His first memory is of shooting Gloria Beatty, 'The impact of the bullet had turned her head a little away from me; I did not have a perfect profile view but I could see enough of her face and her lips to see that she was smiling.' By the end, when this scene is replayed, we understand why Gloria was smiling and why Robert pulled the trigger.

The setting is 1930s Hollywood. The characters are dumb daydreamer Robert and hardbitten, gloomy Gloria who meet and become friends. Gloria says that she has tried to kill herself in Dallas because her life has been so bad, but the doctors saved her. She wonders why "everybody pays so much attention to living and so little to dying." Gloria suggests they enter the dance marathon because they are fed, and they get $1,000 if they win. More importantly, there are usually directors and producers in the audience who could spot them and make them stars. The marathon is held in a dance hall on a pier. This rat race to live, to keep moving, to keep yourself busy so that you survive, becomes an allegory for the passage of life, and hence a race towards death rather than from it. Gloria says, "This whole business is a merry-go-round. Once we get out of here we're right back where we started."

As we become embroiled in the marathon (there are 15-minute elimination races each day, an old woman Mrs Layden gets sponsorship for them, Mario is arrested for murder) it becomes apparent that Gloria is becoming more distant. While Robert seeks the sunlight coming through the skylight, Gloria stays in the shadows. Mrs Layden advises Robert to stay away from Gloria who is no good and will only drag him down - she holds him back literally during the elimination races. Just as things are looking up for Robert (he talks to film director Frank Borzage, Mrs Layden reveals she is rich, Mr Maxwell of Jonathan Beer is about to give him his big break) there is an argument, shots are fired, a man lies dead. Mrs Layden is killed by a stray bullet. Gloria wishes it had been her. The contest is called off with the money equally divided between the remaining couples.

Gloria and Robert walk out into the darkness - it is after 2 in the morning. Gloria is fed up with this stinking life. Robert tells her that she has to stop thinking that way. Before he met her, he always thought of succeeding. He had never thought of failing before he met her. Realising the effect she has on people, Gloria says that she is no good, that she wished she had died in Dallas. Robert thinks: yes, that would have been better. Gloria takes out a pistol. (She must have had it for a long time, just waiting.) "Shoot me. It's the only way to get me out of my misery." Robert remembers the time his grandfather had to put down Nellie, their workhorse. "It was the kindest thing to do. She was no more good." Robert picks up the pistol and shoots Gloria. And seals his own death sentence.

Born on April 14 1897 in Pegram near Nashville, Tennessee, Horace Stanley McCoy began work as a newsboy at the age of 12, and held a succession of jobs (salesman, taxi driver). During World War One, he served in the US Air Service as a bombardier and aerial photographer. During an attack by 4 German Fokkers, he was wounded and his crew killed, but still he managed to shoot down a fighter and fly the plane home. For his bravery, he was awarded the Croix de Guerre. McCoy became the sports and crime writer for the *Dallas Dispatch*, and then sports editor at the *Dallas Journal* in 1920. He was 6 foot 4 inches, had an athletic body, won local golf and handball championships, was expert at tennis, and used his sports writing position to further his social climbing. To supplement his high living, McCoy began writing for *Black Mask* in 1927. With mounting debts, he left his job and became editor of the literary magazine *The Dallasite*. It soon folded and he ran off which a rich girl - the marriage was quickly annulled. (These experiences became the background to *No Pockets In A Shroud* (1937), an 'autobiographical' novel about a crusading reporter and his affairs.) Needing cash, McCoy knuckled down to writing for the pulps. His acting in The Dallas Little Theatre got some attention so McCoy moved to Los Angeles in 1931 for a screen test. He failed. This period of trying to make it in the movies was used as background for *I Should Have Stayed Home* (1938), McCoy's masterpiece of low-life actors and actresses in parasitic Hollywood. McCoy became a road bum, and submitted story ideas to the studios. One, called *Marathon Dancers*, eventually became *They Shoot Horses, Don't They?* In 1932, he got a contract writing B-movies and began a long career of writing such films. Although his novels were scarcely noticed in America, the French recognised his existential angst and ranked him along with Hemingway, Steinbeck and Faulkner. Next came a brute of a crime novel, *Kiss Tomorrow Goodbye* (1948), the story of an intelligent, ambitious, sadistic crook. It was followed by *Scalpel* (1952), a book about an ambitious surgeon. McCoy was beginning to make a lot of money, and write/direct a film when he had a fatal heart attack on December 15 1955. A book based on a film outline, *Corruption City*, was published in 1959.

The problem with being creative is that we live in a society where we are taught from an early age to want fame and fortune, yet at the same time the artist wants to be taken seriously. This causes tension because rarely does serious thought lead to big bucks. Horace McCoy was torn apart by this problem because he was brought up in a household which was money poor and book rich. Throughout his life he fraternised with the rich and made money from writing film scripts, whilst aspiring to make something worthwhile with his novels. This tension is perfectly realised in his novels which are about people who aspire to great wealth/recognition and at the same time despise everything that it stands for.

Fear (1940-1949)

Gerald Butler wrote 6 novels, starting with *Kiss The Blood Off My Hands* (1940), an enormous best-seller with over 250,000 sales in hardback. The story is simple - an American conman in London gets into a rage, kills a man, and goes on the run, finds refuge in a woman's room, holds her hostage, they fall in love, he tries to reform, circumstances conspire against them and they both go on the run. The novel is a fever dream, like Steve Fisher's *I Wake Up Screaming*, published a year later in America. The most shocking thing about it is the ending. When our lovelorn couple are about to be caught, the beautiful heroine is horribly disfigured in an automobile accident. As it turns out, they are not apprehended and after the heroine recovers they escape to France unhindered. They live a life of domesticity on a farm.

All his novels (*They Cracked Her Glass Slipper* (1942); *Their Rainbow Had Black Edges* (1943); *Mad With Much Heart* (1947); *Slippery Hitch* (1949); *Choice Of Two Women/Blow Hot, Blow Cold* (1951); and *There Is A Death, Elizabeth* (1972)) deal with obsession - men for women and women for men. When people are in love, to what lengths will they go? These books get darker and darker. The violence becomes more psychological. Hard choices have to be made. There are no easy solutions. The central characters are in a constant state of fear. Fear that a lover will betray them. Fear of being alone. Fear of staying together.

With the outbreak of World War Two, there was a lot of fear around, which pervaded Noir Fiction. Horrified by the war, either through personal experience or through their friends' tales, the absurdity of life on this planet was becoming all too obvious.

39

From France, we heard the rational voices of Albert Camus and Boris Vian. From America, John Franklin Bardin, William Lindsay Gresham and Cornell Woolrich fuelled their writing with their nightmares. In the UK, Gerald Butler, Patrick Hamilton and Gerald Kersh furnished disparate ideas.

Albert Camus: A Dark Wind Blowing From The Future

It is common for Jean-Paul Sartre and Albert Camus to be mentioned in the same breath as Existentialism. This is the same mistake as linking Dashiell Hammett with James M Cain and calling them Hard-Boiled. Sartre was an Existentialist - he believed that people were defined by their actions. Everybody has control over their lives, and the freedom to evaluate every situation before making a choice. Since man is always reinventing himself by his choices, he can only be known by his actions. This is quite similar to a Hard-Boiled point of view - the private eye observes the actions of others and divines their character from these actions.

Camus on the other hand took the point of view of the absurdists. He believed that things existed without explanation or reason, so our own existence is equally absurd. If we cannot find a purpose for our existence, then we can fall into a profoundly dark and solitary anguish.

We are in an abyss. Some people prefer to be pessimists, to look no further than the abyss, so they swim in their own morbid self-indulgence. Others accept the abyss, and see that they are free to transform themselves by their actions, like Existentialists. However, there are others who abdicate from their freedom by acting out their lives as others expect, so that they can feel safe and secure.

Jean-Paul Sartre (1905-1980) (*Nausea* (1938)) and Albert Camus (1913-1960) (*The Outsider* (1942)) wrote many nerve-tingling novels about the actions and thoughts of their characters, using some of the conventions of the Hard-Boiled and Noir writers they admired. Both Horace McCoy's *They Shoot Horses, Don't They?* and James M Cain's *The Postman Always Rings Twice* use the same 'confession' framing device as *The Outsider*. It is probable that they were an influence.

The Outsider is the story of Patrice Meursault, a shipping clerk. It is set in Algeria and begins with the death of Meursault's mother. He travels to the nursing home where she lived - he could not afford to look after her at his apartment and besides they were not close. When he arrives, the casket is covered, and he is not interested in seeing her face, so the cover is not removed. During the all-night vigil, accompanied by his mother's friends, he smokes and drinks coffee. The next day, for the funeral, they walk a long way to the cemetery in tremendous heat. He does not ask when she died. He does not know how old she is. He does not cry or show emotion.

The following day, Saturday, Meursault goes swimming, meets Marie and makes love to her. On Sunday, he stays in and watches the world go by from his window. 'Really, nothing in my life had changed.'

Raymond, one of Meursault's neighbours, becomes friendly. He gets Meursault to write out a letter for him, which would tell off Raymond's girlfriend. Later, Raymond is heard beating his girlfriend and the police are called. Meursault goes to the police and acts as a witness for Raymond - saying that the girl had done wrong by Raymond.

Masson, a friend of Raymond's, invites Raymond, Meursault and Marie to his beach house for the weekend. They are a happy crowd. There are a couple of unhappy Arabs hanging around, the brother and friend of Raymond's girlfriend. There is a confrontation - Raymond is badly cut in the arm and mouth. The Arabs run off.

While Masson and Raymond go to a doctor, Meursault stares at the sea and walks on the beach. He comes across the Arab who knifed Raymond, lying in the shade. The sun is beating down on Meursault, the same sun that beat down on his mother's funeral. He steps forward to get out of the sun, the Arab gets out his knife, Meursault shoots him. Then shoots him 4 more times.

Meursault is sentenced to death because he did not show remorse at his mother's funeral, and because he associated with Raymond (who may have been a pimp but it is not proved). It is an absurd situation. Meursault is condemned to death because he refuses to live as a hypocrite, to behave as society expects. Living in his cell, Meursault thinks all the time. The examining magistrate and the priest try to impose God upon Meursault and he nods and pays lip-service to what they say to get rid of them. Then, before his execution, he snaps. He has had enough of the hypocrisy. He tells the priest that God does not exist, that there is no afterlife, that 'nothing, nothing had the least importance.' He is indifferent to his death sentence because every man is a condemned man. Every man is living under a death sentence. The knowledge of our inescapable death was 'the dark wind' blowing from our future. The goals/hopes one sets oneself, the importance one gives to things - all this is derisory in the face of the truth. If so, then why play the social game? Life is absurd. Meursault was happy with this knowledge, because he could begin each day afresh, enjoying the 'benign indifference of the universe,' much as Dostoyevsky discovered the joy of living life to the full at his execution.

Written in the first person, we do not learn much about Meursault because he does not know himself. He experiences life, enjoys it, takes pleasure in it, without anxiety or stress. He tells us about it in a detached manner because he is concerned with absolute truth. The people and the world exist. He accepts them in all their pain, suffering, joy and absurdity. They are all equal to him. He is tolerant of their lies. Even in prison, he accepts the life he is forced to lead. At the end, he becomes angry with the priest because he cannot tolerate the lies any more. In shouting at the priest, he reveals to the priest, to the reader, and to himself, his understanding of life, his refusal to accept anything but the absolute truth.

The events and settings are based upon events in the lives of Camus' friends. For example, when commiserating with painter Sauveur Galliero over the recent death of the painter's mother, Galliero said that after he buried his mother he went to the movies with his woman. It is no wonder that one of the working titles for the book was *L'Indifférent/Indifference*. Camus' friend Pierre Galindo was both part Meursault and part Raymond - a similar event to the knife fight on the beach actually occurred to him near Oran in Algeria.

Published by Gallimard in an edition of 4,400 copies on June 15 1942, *L'Etranger* was one part of an absurd trilogy written by Camus. *The Myth Of Sisyphus*, published later in 1942, says that only one question is worth asking: Is life worth living? If so, then what do we live for? The final part of the trilogy was the play *Caligula*, written in 1939 and published in 1944.

Born in Algeria on November 13 1913, and growing up French in a Moslem land, Albert Camus felt alienated. He had many jobs (including a goalkeeper for the Algiers football team) before becoming a journalist in France. He was active in the French Resistance during World War Two, and edited the secret newspaper *Combat*. With the publication of *L'Etranger* and *The Myth Of Sisyphus* in 1942, he became established on the literary scene and turned to writing full time. Camus was awarded the Nobel Prize for Literature in 1957, before dying in a car crash in 1960.

John Franklin Bardin: Then Something Snapped Inside Me

Each of John Franklin Bardin's three great Noir novels begin with a weird, whimsical and, at the same time, worrying situation. He then spends the next 200 pages explaining how the surreal is real, and that abnormal psychology is a normal state for most people. Along the way, his central characters doubt the reality of their circumstances, break away from their normal lives and see the world in a different light. In Bardin's books the insane are the most normal people you are likely to meet.

In the UK, he was admired by the likes of Kingsley Amis, Edmund Crispin, Roy Fuller and Julian Symons (the latter supplying an illuminating introduction in the 1976 collection of the three great works). Symons compared Bardin to Edgar Allan Poe (for the hallucinogenic nature of the stories) and Patricia Highsmith (for treating abnormal psychology as an everyday occurrence) and I cannot help but agree with him.

In *The Deadly Percheron* (Dodd, US, 1946), a pleasant young man, Jacob Blunt, walks into the office of psychiatrist Dr George Matthews and, after a short conversation, is relieved to find out he is mad. The reason? A little man is giving Jacob $10 a day to wear a flower in his hair. Another little man is paying him $10 a day to give away $20 in quarters. Yet another pays for him to whistle at Carnegie Hall during performances. Jacob fears that if it is all true, then leprechauns and fairies and elves and goblins really do exist. Dr Matthews decides to accompany Jacob and finds too much of his story to be true. Dr Matthews begins to doubt his own sanity and he knows that is not such a good thing for a psychiatrist. Then, he is knocked out, awakes maybe a year later, in hospital, finds he has a new identity, and must prove himself to be compos mentis. He becomes a different man to get out of hospital. As John Brown, looking like someone who has seen better days, he gets a job as a waiter and busboy. Then he is run down by a car and his face is horribly disfigured. It is as though his mind and body were being slowly chopped away to find out what he is really made of. And then things take a turn for the worst.

Dr Matthews also turns up as a supporting character in Bardin's next book. *The Last Of Philip Banter* (Dodd, US, 1947) has a great premise that could easily have been borrowed by Italo Calvino or Paul Auster. An advertising executive, Philip Banter, is under a lot of pressure at work, has a drink problem and a difficult wife. He arrives at work and finds a small pile of paper on his desk. The manuscript, supposedly written by him the next day tells, in retrospect, the events of that day. It gives his most innermost thoughts. As the day progresses, the events in the manuscript unfold in minute detail. The same thing happens the next day. And the day after that. The manuscript is frighteningly accurate and Philip Banter dreads going into the office to discover what new horrors await him. The novel follows Banter's mental disintegration.

Both these novels are suffused with a feeling of helplessness. For all of Dr Matthews' efforts, for all of his knowledge and intelligence and ingenuity, in the end he fails at every point to prevent the deaths occurring around him.

Written in six weeks, taken from an agent's office by Victor Gollancz and published without revision, *Devil Take The Blue-Tail Fly* (Gollancz , UK, 1948) is a white-heat, fever-dream of a novel that constantly keeps you on your toes. It begins with Ellen in her cell, in a mental institution. Today is the day, the day she is going home. She has to be careful. She has to watch what she says and does in front of everybody. They must think that she is normal. She knows that she is normal, but they do not. She must not do anything which makes them suspicious.

When she is released, Ellen returns to her husband Basil, and returns to reality. Only, something is not quite right. There is something askew with the world. Ellen is a musician. She plays a harpsichord. She is highly strung. There is her doctor, Dr Danzer, to whom she recounts her dreams.

This novel is about the pain of creation, and the joy of destruction. It is a dance, a dance of death. It soon becomes apparent who is Ellen's dancing partner - herself. Or rather, her other self.

It is a story told to a slow beat and its tense atmosphere is reminiscent of Roman Polanski's film *Repulsion* (1965).

Born November 30 1916 in Cincinnati, Ohio, after attending high school, Bardin began at the University of Cincinnati. However, misfortune devastated the family. An elder sister died of septicaemia, and his father (a coal merchant by trade) died of a coronary. With no money to support the family, Bardin was forced to leave the University during his first year and get a regular job as a ticket taker and bouncer at a roller rink. He was there for four years. "I believe that the social contact with thousands of people a night helped me to become a writer and possibly offset my lack of a college education," he told *Contemporary Authors*. What he did not tell that illustrious institution was that by this time his mother has become a paranoid schizophrenic. "It was on visits to her that I first had an insight into the 'going home' hallucinations," he told Julian Symons, referring to Ellen's thoughts at the beginning of *Devil Take The Blue-Tail Fly*.

While working at a bookshop during the day, Bardin spent his nights educating himself and reading. He cited his influences as Graham Greene, Henry Green and Henry James. Although one can see the energy and perversion of some of Graham Greene's 'entertainments' - *Brighton Rock*, for example - in Bardin's work, it is hard to discern anything more from his preferred reading matter.

In 1943, Bardin joined the Edwin Bird Wilson advertising agency, established himself financially, married and had two children. It was during this period that he began his feverish writing, resulting in his Noir trilogy being published over 18 months. Looking back, one can see how each book became more personal - the first is surreal, the second is the mental disintegration of an advertising executive and the third a mad woman's descent into schizophrenia.

Over the next 20 years, he rose to the position of vice-president and member of board of directors of Edwin Bird Wilson. Towards the end of this period, from 1961 to 66, Bardin ran a writers' workshop at New York's New School For Social Research. He also divorced and remarried. Bardin concentrated on editorial duties (senior editor at Coronet from 1968 to 72, then managing editor of *Today's Health* (1972 to 73) and *Barrister And Learning And The Law* (1973 to 74)) and then had a seven-year period as a freelance writer before dying in New York on July 9 1981.

After his 'black' novels Bardin wrote *The Burning Glass* (Scribner, US, 1950) which intriguingly opens with a character suffocating inside a coffin. The book is a day in the life of free-living, irresponsible artists and intellectuals at a summer colony. Their behaviour is copied and commented upon by a 12-year-old boy, which Bardin uses to both comic and horrific effect. He followed this with the overly sentimental *Christmas Comes But Once A Year* (Scribner, US, 1953). Between their publications, Bardin was very prolific, writing novels as Douglas Ashe (*A Shroud For Grandmama* (Scribner, US, 1951), also published as *The Long-Street Legacy* (Paperback Library, US, 1970)) and Gregory Tree (*The Case Against Myself* (Scribner, US, 1950), *The Case Against Butterfly* (Scribner, US, 1951) and *So Young To Die* (Scribner, US, 1953)). These also feature some dark and wondrous characters, but they fail to capture the Noir edge of his first three efforts.

After Julian Symons tracked down Bardin to ask him questions for Penguin's 1976 Omnibus edition of Bardin's three Noir novels, Bardin decided to work on another novel. The result was the difficult to find *Purloining Tiny* (Harper, US, 1978).

Bardin told *Contemporary Authors*, "There is only one motive for writing a novel: to be published and read. To me there is no distinction between the mystery novel and the novel, only between good books and bad books. A good book takes the reader into a new world of experience; it is an experiment. A bad book, unless the writing is inept, reinforces the intransigent attitude of the reader not to experiment with a new world." As well written as his other novels were, they could not compare to the touch of personal agony that he brought to his early work.

William Lindsay Gresham:
Nothing Matters In This Goddamned Lunatic Asylum Of A World But Dough

Imagine a world obsessed by the acquisition of money. One man finds out what you need, preys on this weakness to get money out of you, and then moves onto bigger and bigger fish. Only, there are other people like this man. What happens when he meets someone who preys on his weaknesses?

Nightmare Alley (1946) is the story of Stanton Carlisle. He begins at the carnival by helping out at the Ten-in-One tent, giving the geek his chicken. Stan is happy with the shiny half-dollar in his trouser pocket and plays with it. And then he gets the idea that he should have more shiny new coins. And girls. He beds women to get what he wants. He learns the codes to become a mentalist - the person talking to the blindfolded mentalist nonchalantly includes code words into their speech, which identify the necessary objects. Stan wants to go even further, to aim for bigger stakes, more affluent marks.

So he decorates a parlour and sets himself up as a spiritualist - a popular occupation which satisfied the need of many who wanted to talk to dead sons after the wholesale slaughter of World War One. With each move up the social ladder, Stan finds another woman with whom to cohabit - they give him their confidences, their secrets and he makes profit out of them.

This is the world of the con. The magicians, the mentalists, the spiritualists and the psychiatrists are fakes. Only the freaks of nature are real people. Gresham uses the carnival people as a cross-section of society. The giant Hercules embodies the lumpen proletariat who know they are being screwed but do nothing about it. Major Mosquite is the little bit of pure hate we keep in our hearts - all talk and no action. Joe Plasky, the man with no legs, is the man of action. Mary is a passive woman who allows Stan to abuse her. Zeena, the mistress, is desire - she is the one who shows Stan that the only way forward in the world is through deception. And then there is Dr Lilith Ritter, a woman who shoehorns her way into the spiritualist racket and takes control of Stan. Together, they strip society bare.

But every predator in the food chain sooner or later becomes the prey, which Stan discovers to his cost. It takes him a much shorter time to slide down than it did to go up. In the end, Stan ends up as the lowest of the low, the plankton of the food chain - a geek.

Gresham's only other novel was *Limbo Tower* (1949) an equally down-beat work about Asa Kimball and other men slowly dying of fear, depression, disease and tuberculosis in hospital. He is well known in magic circles for his biography of *Houdini: The Man Who Walked Through Walls* (1959), and his non-fiction book about freak shows and carnivals, *Monster Midway* (1953). Gresham supported himself with a regular flow of short stories and articles in *Ellery Queen's Mystery Magazine*, *Esquire* and other publications. If there was a book about carnivals, circuses and freaks that needed reviewing for the *New York Times*, Gresham was usually assigned the job.

Born in Baltimore on August 20 1909, William Lindsay Gresham was the descendant of a family that settled in Maryland in 1641. His father needed to pursue a factory job so the family moved to New York. On a visit to the freak show at Coney Island, the young Gresham became fascinated by a sharply-dressed, suave-looking Italian man, who had a small headless body hanging out of his stomach. The small body was also impeccably dressed. Learning that the Italian was happily married with 5 normal children, Gresham began to envy him - all Gresham had was a father afraid of losing his job and a mother always grousing about money.

After jobs as a stenographer and freelance reporter, Gresham ended up in Greenwich Village singing folk music at a bohemian nightspot. He met a wealthy woman and married her. Then in November 1936, like many idealistic young men during the turbulent 1930s he joined the Communist Party, taking the name William Rafferty. In November 1937, after a close friend died at Brunete, Gresham went to Spain and fought, with the Abraham Lincoln Battalion, on the side of the Republicans in the Spanish Civil War.

Gresham was a foot soldier, a topographer and then a first aider. It was in the latter post that he met a medic who liked to reminisce about his times in a carnival. This was Joseph Daniel 'Doc' Halliday, a former seaman and male nurse. It was from him that Gresham learned all about the carny culture, the habits, the mentality, the language. And it was there that he first came across the word geek. It referred to the lowest of the low - an alcoholic or drug addict who was out of his head all the time. He could be prodded, cajoled and led into working for more drink or drugs. His job? To sit and crawl in his own excrement, as the wild man of Borneo or some such, and occasionally bite the heads off chickens and snakes. Immediately, a story idea entered into Gresham's head, about the rise of a carny conman and his subsequent descent into geekdom.

When Gresham returned to New York, his marriage collapsed and ended in divorce. He took to drink and, in despair, attempted to hang himself in a closet but the hook came loose and he fell to the ground, gaining consciousness hours later. To repair his mind, he went to psychoanalysis. To keep his body occupied, he worked as a salesman, magician, copywriter and magazine editor. Then he married again, to the writer and poetess Helen Joy Davidman, by whom he had two sons, David and Douglas.

With stories and articles being published regularly, Gresham began work on his novel, hanging out at the Dixie Hotel, where the carnival workers did their drinking. Gresham published *Nightmare Alley* in 1946 and it met with immediate and large sales success. It also sold to Hollywood for $60,000 and became a very good Film Noir the following year. With the proceeds of this success, Gresham moved to a large estate in Staatsburg, about 75 miles north of New York City.

While Gresham was writing the equally bleak *Limbo Tower* (1949), both Joy and Gresham left the Communist Party and found religion. They joined the Presbyterian church. Gresham probably believed he was on the road to a successful career as a novelist, but that was not to be the case. The funds began to dry up, resulting in strained arguments between husband and wife. Another cause of tension was that Gresham did not believe he should sleep with only one woman. Joy believed otherwise.

Cracking under the pressure, Gresham began drinking heavily and would fly into rages for little or no reason. One time he broke a bottle over Douglas' head. Chairs were regularly broken against the pillars on the front of the house. Gresham dabbled in Zen, the tarot, Yoga, I Ching and Dianetics to soothe his personal demons with little success.

Then in 1952 Joy became very ill and was advised by her doctor to plan a long vacation. Around this time, Joy's first cousin, Renée Rodriguez, visited

Staatsburg to hide herself and her two children from her abusive husband, Claude Pierce. (Haunted by his experiences during World War Two, Claude began to drink, became abusive and treated Renée like a slave.) With someone to look after Gresham, Joy went on vacation, and left for England in August 1952. Gresham wrote to Joy in January 1953 saying that he and Renée had become lovers. Joy returned immediately. There were arguments, tears, rages and finally divorce. Joy sold the house to pay off the Internal Revenue Service and moved to England with the boys. In 1956, she married author C S Lewis and died tragically on July 14 1960. Their relationship was the basis of the stage play and film *Shadowlands*.

Gresham moved to Florida with Renée and they were married in 1954 - Gresham joined Alcoholics Anonymous and seemed to find some sort of peace. Shortly after Joy's death, Gresham visited England to see his sons. When it became apparent that they were well cared for, he left them in C S Lewis' care. Reflecting on his life, Gresham told a fellow veteran from Spain, "I sometimes think that if I have any real talent it is not literary but is a sheer talent for survival. I have survived three busted marriages, losing my boys, war, tuberculosis, Marxism, alcoholism, neurosis and years of freelance writing. Just too mean and ornery to kill, I guess."

Gresham discovered he had cancer of the tongue. He had no wish for either he or his family to face a long, ugly death, so on September 14 1962 he checked into the run-down Dixie Hotel room, registering as 'Asa Kimball, of Baltimore,' and took his own life. The only tribute paid to him in the *New York Times* came from the bridge columnist.

Boris Vian:
I Was Sorry I Hadn't Been Able To Bring Her
One Of Her Sister's Eyes

Paris. Summer 1946. Jean d'Halluin wanted to launch his new press, Editions du Scorpion, with a best-seller, so he asked his friend Boris Vian if he knew any good Hard Boiled American writers he could publish. Vian said that he'd just translated a book by Vernon Sullivan, a black American who couldn't get the book published in America because of the racist overtones. The title was *J'irai cracher sur vos tombes (I Spit On Your Graves)*.

The story is about Lee Anderson, who enters the small town of Buckton, and takes over the management of the local bookstore. To make sure he gets sales, he must use all the sales literature sent by head office (the most salacious titles get the most publicity), he must skim the new books so that he knows what they are about, he must remember the names of everyone in town and he must go to church.

Making a good living, Lee decides to find out where the local girls hang out. Being, slightly older, blond, muscled, a good dancer, a singer and guitarist, with an ample supply of liquor, he is immediately welcome in the small group. Lee is driven to seek women and to screw them at every opportunity. They are happy to fall into his arms and to take everything he can give.

Only, Lee is black, a mulatto who passes for white, and he's seeking revenge on white people for the death of his brother. With this in mind, he finds two rich sisters, and decides he will seduce each in turn, humiliate them, then kill them.

Paris. November 1946. In France, immediately after the war, everything American was great. The Film Noirs of the war years which had been banned by the Germans, were grabbing the public's attention. Marcel Duhamel started his Serie Noire line of American Hard Boiled translations at Gallimard. Only not many people seemed to be that interested in Vernon Sullivan. What the book needed was publicity. It got it, in spades.

February 1947. Daniel Parker, head of a right-wing moral action group, who was already fighting the depraved works of Henry Miller, decided that *J'irai cracher sur vos tombes* was equally depraved. Many people had never heard about this depraved work and decided to find out for themselves just how depraved it was.

April 1947. A salesman in Paris went mad and strangled his girlfriend in a hotel room. Beside her lifeless body, he left a copy of the book. He had circled certain passages describing the death of one of the rich sisters by strangulation. It was a scandal. Everyone wanted to know more about the murder, and about the book that inspired it.

Jean d-Halluin printed lots more copies, outselling French favourites Sartre and Camus in 1947, and had sold half a million by 1950. Boris Vian made a lot of money from it too, and some notoriety, because by 1948 it had been revealed that there was no such person as Vernon Sullivan and that Vian was the real author.

Rather than find and translate an American crime thriller, which would have been too much work, Vian had gone on his traditional family holiday to Vendée on August 5 1946 and, in ten days, had written the book. The American pseudonym had come from Vian's friend Paul Vernon and the jazz pianist Joe Sullivan. The original title was *I Dance On Your Graves*, but his wife didn't think it was gritty enough, so 'Dance' was changed to 'Spit.' Although Vian had never been to America, he had learnt a lot about racial prejudice and attitudes from black American jazz musicians he played with - Vian was a well-known jazz trumpeter on the Parisian cabaret circuit.

When Vian was brought to court by Daniel Parker for translating "objectionable foreign literature," Vian collaborated with Milton Rosenthal on an English-language version, published by Vendome Press in April 1948, to 'prove' that Vernon Sullivan was real, and deflect attention away from Vian. It didn't work - the cat was out of the bag and, in 1951, Vian was fined one hundred thousand francs.

Boris Vian wrote four other 'translations' of Vernon Sullivan, which didn't have the same impact as the first novel but still sold a fair amount. (Much like James Hadley Chase and *No Orchids For Miss Blandish*.) Ironically, it was as a result of *I Spit On Your Graves*, that he got offered work to do real translations - his first book being *The Big Clock* by Kenneth Fearing. After that came other crime author translations like Peter Cheyney, before diversifying with translations of Nelson Algren A E van Vogt, August Strindberg and, most appropriately, Richard Wright.

Born March 10 1920 near Paris, and brought up in comfortable surroundings, at the age of twelve Boris Vian contracted rheumatic fever, which left him with a chronic heart condition. He was told that he could die at any time and would certainly not live past the age of forty. Unsurprisingly, this had a profound effect on the way he lived his life, and the subjects he wrote about. Life and death co-existed in his life and work.

Always conscious of the lack of time he had to do anything, Vian threw himself into everything he did. His daytime job was as an engineer. After hearing Duke Ellington's orchestra in Paris, Vian took up the trumpet despite medical advice against it. When he was twenty-two, he was performing with the Claude Abadie orchestra. He worked to all hours.

Vian was a surrealist, a pataphysician, an absurdist. He became the closest French friend of Duke Ellington, Miles Davis and Charlie Parker, and was friends with the leading authors (Jean-Paul Sartre, Simone de Beauvoir) who got his short stories into the influential magazine *Temps moderne*.

He wrote two unpublished novels before he got his break with *I Spit On Your Graves*. And after the crime books and translations his more personal work began to appear. Such was his output, that many of these were not published until after his death.

After the publication of what many regard as his best book *L'ecume des jours* (published in English as *Froth On The Daydream* and *Mood Indigo*) in 1947, Vian gave up the day job and concentrated on writing full-time. *L'ecume des jours* is a tragic love story set in a world where figures of speech assume literal reality, and familiar objects fight back surrealistically. Streets are named after jazz figures Sidney Bichet and Louis Armstrong; Colin, the hero, has a "100,000 doublezoons" before dinner, Colin and Chloe drink "pianococktails" created by a machine which mixes exotic drinks according to the music of Duke Ellington; Chloe becomes fatally stricken when a water-lily grows on her lung. There being no money for a funeral, the undertaker throws her coffin out the window, where it strikes an innocent child and breaks her leg.

He wrote four hundred songs. Dozens of books. Hundreds of articles. Poems. Plays. Libretto for opera. His pseudonyms include Baron Visi, Adolph Schmurz, and Bison Ravi. All were full of spontaneous humour, and violence.

In *Papers on Language and Literature*, Jennifer Walters observed that, 'the central theme of Vian's prose work is the way man moves incessantly and irrevocably toward death. His books are liberally bestrewn with corpses of all kinds, and rare is the story which does not end with the death of one or more of the protagonists.'

Vian knew he was going to die, but was going to do what he wanted until that time came. There were no boundaries for him, and his characters reflect this attitude. In *I Spit On You Graves*, Lee Anderson has no moral compunctions. He screws women and under-age girls. He gets them drunk so that he can screw them. At one stage, he says of Jean Asquith, one of the rich sisters, 'I never had any luck with her. Always sick, either from having drunk too much or screwed too much.'

So what is the point of the book?

Vian wants to shock us, to create a mini-earthquake in our heads. He doesn't hide what people can be like. If you go into a bar, you are going to see a lot of young men and women getting drunk and eyeing each other up, to see who they want to get laid by. Vian shows this. The characters are not worried about this behaviour - it's natural to them. What is shocking is the way Vian writes about it. The language is terse, direct, concise. He doesn't pull punches.

In 1959, a film version of *I Spit On Your Graves* was made, which Vian did not want to be associated with. Watching a preview, as the opening frames flickered on the screen, he commented, "These guys are supposed to be American? My ass!.." and his heart stopped. He was only thirty-nine.

Gerald Kersh: In Every Man There Lurks A Hungry Beast

For every successful author, there are a thousand others struggling to get in print. Gerald Kersh was one of those word hustlers who haunted all night coffee bars in London's Soho, writing on stolen toilet paper, making a mug last until daybreak. And when he made it, when he became one of England's highest paid wordsmiths, fate and circumstance cruelly ganged up to throw him back in the gutter.

Night And The City (1938) is a novel of disgust. Of all Kersh's novels, it is the one where you most feel the fetid stink of the city, and the worthless lives of the people in it. As one reviewer put it, 'This novel of the London under-world has something of the realism of a Hogarth picture and the satire of a Swift. Pimps, prostitutes, panderers, petty crooks and odd characters move about in low joints and night clubs, fleecing and being fleeced by each other.'

The first third of the novel introduces us to Harry Fabian, and his efforts to make money. Sauntering down a Soho street in his sharp suit, Fabian, cultivates an American accent, and talks in terms of dollars instead of pounds. This is ponce (pimp) Harry Fabian, who lives on the immoral earnings of Zoë, his girl, a lovely streetwalker (prostitute) of 23 who, at present, can make money easily. Harry is under the impression he is so clever nobody can see through him. As it says in the novel, '…he fools nobody as completely as he fools himself…' Basically, he is a loser. Harry puts a proposition to Figler to start their own wrestling circus, but Harry has to come up with his half of £100, otherwise the deal is off. We tour the high and (mostly) low spots of Soho with Fabian who 'saw London as a kind of Inferno- a series of concentric areas with Piccadilly Circus as the ultimate centre.' Fabian finds a little old man with Zoë and blackmails him for £110. Fabian is in the wrestling business!

The next section of the book describes how the characters fall into a life of moral turpitude. Helen, a naïve typist, is persuaded by the vile Vi to become a hostess at the Silver Fox club. Vi initiates Helen into the world of low company, where the steps only go down. She does this because the greatest consolation of the degraded human being is the fact that there are others in the same mire. Adam is a big, handsome man who dreams of becoming a sculptor. He gets a job as a waiter at the club. Into the Silver Fox slides Fabian, putting on his American accent and acting the big man (his Achilles heel). He is baited and prodded until he is a drunken shell, cleaned out of every penny he has. He vomits on the street, then slumps into it. Later, while Helen links up with Fabian, becoming more corrupt, Adam begins work on his sculpture.

The last section of the novel is about each character struggling to 'better' themselves. For most of them, the word 'better' means more money. Adam (obviously Kersh's alter ego in the novel) wants to achieve something more important, to make some sculptures, so he leaves his high-paying job at the Silver Fox, and goes to work in his room.

Despite all the wallowing in the smells and sounds of Soho, Kersh is ultimately optimistic about the world and its future: 'All life is a cycle of ripening and decay. The seed which you plant in the soil goes back to the dirt in dung; the seed which you plant in the womb goes back to the earth in abominable putrefaction - yet life stirs in the rottenness; life struggles upwards, from change to change; and death and decay beget higher life. Out of the rottenness of dead leaves creep higher and more fruitful trees. Tree fights tree, until, out of the frenzy of the wrestling jungle climbs the tree that seems to touch the sky. Even the grass strives, blade against blade, towards the sun - rising, falling and growing again. Life moves eternally upwards.'

Richard Church, reviewing *Night And The City* for *John O'London's* (March 25 1938) wrote that 'Only a visionary who feels desperately about the sins of the world could apply the scourge so mercilessly.' And 'It is macabre. It has the horrible fascinated hatred of vice which mediaeval poets from Dante downwards, revelled in and demonstrated with all their rhetorical devices then fashionable. Now rhetoric is too rarely used today. It is a technique too heavy and too large-scale for everyday use. Only a man with the strength of moral fervour can pick it up and use it. Mr Kersh is original today because he is a moral rhetorician.' Kersh's approach is reminiscent of mediaeval theologians who believed that if people did not live a good life, then they would endanger society as a whole.

The novel ends with Adam sculpting a man from clay. A man can rise from the earth, from the dirt beneath his feet. If Adam can rise above his surroundings, then perhaps the other characters will in the future. There is always day after the night. (And there is always night after the day.)

Kersh wrote *Night And The City* using his experiences living and working in Soho. It was a major breakthrough for him both in terms of sales, and for the critical acceptance it garnered him. World War Two interrupted his treatise on morality and the immoral to which he returned in 1947 with the publication of *Prelude To A Certain Midnight*.

A remarkable novel which has curiously been ignored for 50 years, *Prelude To A Certain Midnight* is about the hunt for a child murderer in Soho. The story is told from the point of view of the main characters, jumping back and forth in time and place, ignoring or breaking all the rules of normal storytelling. It is also a sort of deconstruction of the crime and mystery genre.

The formidable do-gooder is represented by Miss Asta Thundersley, who pokes her nose into the case of a murdered little girl, Sonia. She believes that 'Whosoever kicks a dog kicks a man by proxy' because 'if you tear the wings off a fly, then you'll graduate from fly to mouse, mouse to rat, rat to cat, cat to dog, dog to child.' Asta gathers everyone she suspects at a party, and the only thing she learns is how to mix a particularly lethal drink.

The police procedural is in the hands of Detective Inspector 'Dick' Turpin, whose hands find nothing but walls as each clue leads to a dead end. The little girl's family, the Sabitinis, were effectively destroyed by the murder. They never recovered, the father died 6 months later from grief as much as from his ulcer. The mother, needing money, hired out a room to life's natural victim Catchy (who inadvertently helped cause Sonia's death).

The murderer (we see the story from his point of view also) relives the pleasure of killing the little girl, and now knows what Friedrich Nietzsche's Zarathustra meant when he spoke of the murderer who 'thirsted for the pleasure of the knife.' He plans to carry out many more murders, with different instruments, to keep the thrill fresh. And as for the police: 'The danger that followed the kill was, so to speak, the savoury that rounded off the roast.' The murderer blames the murder on his girlfriend, who encouraged him, who made him a man. He dreams of himself as some kind of martyr, full of purity and strength. The murderer is then revealed to be a writer of pulp fiction, where he can turn his sentimental and preposterous daydreams into adolescent fiction.

At the party, Hemmeridge (a writer of mystery novels) says 'one murder makes many.' When we go to a wedding or see a baby, it puts an idea into our head. Likewise with murder - if the murderer gets away with it, it will encourage others to come out of the woodwork and murder likewise. He continues, saying that most of us do our killing vicariously, through books: 'one of those Americanish tough-guy books in which the hero is a bit of a murderer thinly disguised as a private detective and goes about slapping glamorous female prisoners in the face or tearing their clothes off or something.' Monty Bar-Kochba asks why they are so concerned about one child when Hitler has been in power for 2 years, over which time he has raped and murdered 1000s and 1000s of Jewish girls, yet Hitler is received by politicians and there is no uproar. Mr Pink points out that when a murder becomes safe, i.e. when a lynch mob gathers or is made legal, then everybody agrees to and accepts the murder because 'In every man there lurks a hungry beast.'

Emotionally, the book is about the realisation that life is not always what you want it to be, that there are many losers for every winner. And in this story, the only winner is the murderer.

Born August 26 1911 in Teddington-On-Thames, Gerald Kersh grew up in a Jewish family full of 'characters' who were to provide a rich and painful source of literary material in future years. The publication of his first novel *Jews Without Jehovah* (1934) resulted in three uncles and a cousin filing criminal libel suits. A few weeks later, Kersh was involved in a car accident - he was run over by one of his uncles, the car bought on the proceeds of the libel case.

After the success of *Night And The City* (1938) Kersh became well known in Fleet Street as a writer for hire. When the Second World War came, Kersh joined the Coldstream Guards where he wrote a war novel *They Died With Their Boots Clean* (1941) which was one of the best-selling books of the war. War novels flew from his typewriter like bullets from an automatic rifle: *The Nine Lives Of Bill Nelson* (1942), *The Dead Look On* (1943), *A Brain And Ten Fingers* (1943), *Faces In A Dusty Picture* (1944). There were also short story collections, and magazine/newspaper appearances under 5 pseudonyms. From 1941 Kersh wrote as Piers England for *The People*, the largest selling Sunday newspaper during the war with 5½ million copies per week.

Immediately after the war, Kersh visited America and managed to 'crack' the prestigious and high-paying magazines of the day like *The Saturday Evening Post*, *Esquire* and *Collier's*. He should have achieved some sort of fame for his novels *Prelude To A Certain Midnight* (1947), *The Song Of The Flea* (1948) and *The Thousand Deaths Of Mr Small* (1950) but they were largely ignored.

Throughout the war Kersh had written so many books (one every 6 months), articles, poems, film and radio scripts, and short stories, that he only slept 2 hours a night, if he slept at all. He collapsed regularly. The long-predicted breakdown came in 1949, and it haunted him for the rest of his life. Illness began to overtake the body of Kersh. He suffered from malaria, pneumonia, liver infections, diseased cancerous tissue and God knows what else - the result of his travels and, no doubt, his overwork. Most of all he suffered at the hands of his greatest love, his second wife Lee.

Kersh had met Lee, a stunning Canadian newspaper women, in 1939 and left his first wife for her. When Kersh found success in 1941, they moved into progressively bigger suites of rooms in London's exclusive Dolphin Square and travelled the world. Increasingly, they began to quarrel, Lee saying she was bored, Kersh becoming sicker, culminating in the burning-down of their new $20,000 home in Barbados - it was not insured. Lee asked Kersh to leave her alone. Over the next few years Lee systematically fleeced him of all his money, incurred enormous debts for Kersh to pay, made contractual agreements for Kersh and took the advances, stole his antiques, his library of 5000 first editions, and his manuscripts, took a succession of lovers, then sued for divorce and won the case.

Kersh remarried, to Florence Sochis - the woman who saved his life in New York - and settled in various, remote areas of New York State. Always in financial difficulty, their lodgings became more shabby - credit was no longer extended. Both physically and mentally, Kersh was taxed to the limit. From this adversity arose great books: *Fowlers End* (1957), *The Implacable Hunter* (1961) and *The Angel And The Cuckoo* (1966). Kersh died on November 5 1968, suffering from a secondary cancer. He left one manuscript, *Brock* (1969) whose main theme was the treachery within personal relationships - a theme that runs throughout Kersh's work.

Cornell Woolrich:
He's Just A Shadow Walking Around
Without No One To Cast Him

You read. Slowly, painfully, the characters are stretched beyond the limits of your endurance. The air is irrevocably sucked from your lungs. You cough and choke, gasping for oxygen. You need something to take away the tension. There is no relief. You are reading a novel written by Cornell Woolrich.

Compared to the Hard-Boiled writers who relied on short, snappy sentences, characters with cynical attitudes and wisecracking dialogue, Woolrich's writing was sloppy, overblown, convoluted and sometimes purple. Woolrich's approach was more romantic than cynical. His psychological suspense thrillers read like modern day Gothic novels.

One of his major themes was obsessive love. This could be love for somebody who lived (*Phantom Lady* (1942) is about a man sentenced to death for his wife's murder and Carol's race against time to find his alibi), or for somebody who had died (*The Bride Wore Black* (1940) is a relentless revenge thriller about Julie Killeen's cold-blooded murder spree against the men who accidentally killed her husband outside the church on their wedding day).

Another recurring theme was predestination. In *Night Has A Thousand Eyes* (1945), a simple man predicts the death of a millionaire in the jaws of a lion. Having explained what is about to happen, Woolrich slowly and methodically fills in the night's activities with the meticulous accuracy of nightmares. The prose attains a kind of white heat, becomes hot and sticky, as we listen to the people trying to convince themselves that this cannot be happening to them.

Woolrich's stories follow a simple but effective plan. The world falls away from the feet of the central character, and then ordinary events become frightening and grotesque. For example, in one of Woolrich's best novels, *Waltz Into Darkness* (1947), lonely coffee importer Louis Durand marries his pen-pal bride, only to discover she is not his pen pal - she murdered his intended - and then she steals all his money. Louis tracks her down and, rather than kill her, professes his love for her. He is pathetic. It is a sentiment shared by Bonny. Knowing her power over him, she takes advantage of him, strings him along, makes him suffer, and begins to slowly poison him. Upon his death, she suddenly realises that indeed she loved him, but his ears are now deaf to her tearful proclamation.

Woolrich can be melodramatic, and his plots/characters fall apart under close scrutiny, but his words have an uncanny emotional and physical effect.

Cornell George Hopley-Woolrich was born December 4 1903 to Claire and Genaro Hopley-Woolwich. Claire belonged to the cultured and moneyed New York classes, whilst Genaro was an English/Italian civil engineer with an eye for the ladies. In 1907, they resettled in Mexico, but the marriage could not survive the move. Claire returned to New York and it was decided that Cornell would stay with his father until adolescence. The young Cornell travelled around Mexico and Central America with his father, collecting the used rifle shells which littered the streets after Pancho Villa and Carranza had had their latest fight.

It is often stated that Cornell's first encounter with the themes of tragic love and death was when, in 1911, he went to see Puccini's *Madame Butterfly* in Mexico City. Three years later, sitting under the stars, thinking, he suddenly realised that one day he would die and, after that, there was nothing. These thoughts, born under Mexican skies, fed his literature for over 50 years.

Returning to New York in 1918, Cornell or Con, as he was often known, became enmeshed in the excesses of the jazz age. In 1925, Con's heel became infected and he had to stay home from Columbia University. In the almost sexual heat of creation, Con wrote his first novel which was accepted immediately. Reviews of *Cover Charge* (1926), and then *Children Of The Ritz* (1927) compared Con to F Scott Fitzgerald. Con was called to Hollywood in 1928, where he proposed to Violet Stockton, the daughter of movie mogul J Stuart Blackton, who lost all his money in the 1929 stock market crash. The marriage was never consummated and it was over inside 3 months. (In fact, Con was a closet homosexual full of self-loathing.) Con left Hollywood and went back to his mother in New York. He lived in hotel rooms for the rest of his life. During this time he did nothing but work.

Woolrich hammered out short stories for every pulp and magazine he could find (*Black Mask*, *Detective Fiction Weekly*), spewed out novels under pseudonyms (William Irish, George Hopley) as well as under his own name. He wrote a wealth of suspense stories (24 novels and hundreds of short stories), was never out of fashion during his lifetime, sold many of his stories to film and TV companies, and died with a million dollars in the bank. Despite all this recognition, his life remains tantalisingly indistinct. He lived in hotel rooms, chain smoked, drank to excess and tapped away on his Remington typewriter, seemingly oblivious to the outside world. When he did venture into the real world, he often recoiled in fear, allowing his natural paranoia and insecurities to take over. After the death of his mother in 1957, Cornell fell apart. He allowed a foot infection to become gangrenous - it was taken off in 1968. Trapped in a wheelchair (much like the central character of his short story 'Rear Window') he did not finish the year alive. On September 25 1968, he cast no more shadows. Five people attended his funeral.

Paranoia (1950-1959)

The 1950s paperback explosion produced dozens of top-notch Noir writers who explored every possible plot permutation for the tough private eye, the rogue cop, the ruthless reporter, the innocent bystander and the sympathetic killer. These writers include Harry Whittington (1915-1989) (*Fires That Destroy* (1951), *A Ticket To Hell* (1960)) and Dan J Marlowe (*The Name Of The Game Is Death* (1962), *Strongarm* (1963), *Never Live Twice* (1964)). Other writers, like Gil Brewer (1922-1983) (*13 French Street* (1951), *The Red Scarf* (1958)) and Vin Packer (*Spring Fire* (1952), *The Damnation Of Adam Blessing* (1961)), were more forthright about the sexual motives of their characters. In their stories, sex is often used by one character to control another.

In the quiet desperation of the Cold War culture, everybody walked around nonchalantly, looking good, being prosperous, smiling at each other. But behind that smile was the stench of death eating away at their insides. This hypocrisy - do what people expect you to do whilst actually thinking something else - found perhaps its most perfect form in the fiction of Jim Thompson. David Karp took a more confrontational approach to hypocrisy, writing about characters who lock horns with the evils of society. And David Goodis? His characters do not want to be part of society - they want to be left alone to wallow in self-pity. They know that the world is going to continue kicking them in the balls no matter what they try to do.

Jim Thompson: I've Been Dead A Long Time

Jim Thompson (1906-1977) wrote the funniest psycho-killer novels you're ever likely to come across. He successfully combines a heady brew of sex and violence, sadism and humour. His characters are the most vicious, the most unsympathetic, the most amoral you will come across in Noir Fiction. They are trapped by women, by society, but mostly by themselves - the thing inside them that makes them the way they are. These 'things' inside his characters are unmentionable thoughts and feelings that we all have but are afraid to express, or even acknowledge. They are 'the sickness,' or simply 'problems.' Thompson does the unpermissable by making us think these thoughts and feel these feelings. We feel the pain of his grotesque characters, and sometimes even like them in spite of ourselves. Sometimes they die, sometimes they stagnate, and sometimes (although rarely) they redeem themselves; you never know until the end. And at the end, you feel a great sense of relief that the compulsion to read Thompson's book has finished.

For me, Thompson's masterpiece (and last great novel) is *Pop 1280* (1964), which is about Nick Corey, the fat, polite, spineless, sloppy, dumb high sheriff of Potts County. Nick tells us that he has 'problems' and they are driving him plumb out of his mind. He is married to mean and vicious Myra. At the beginning, Nick is watching her naked in bed, 'kind of laying on her stomach, so that I couldn't see her face, which made her look a lot better.' They live above the courthouse with Myra's simple-minded brother (and possibly lover) Lennie. Nick has two lovers (for some strange reason, women are attracted to him) Rose Hauck and Amy Mason. Ken Lacey is his best friend.

When somebody says something he disagrees with, Nick's usual non-committal reply is, "I mean, I ain't saying you're wrong but I ain't saying you're right, either." This line epitomises the character - he is controlling himself, keeping himself in balance. Ironically, his job is to keep the world equalised, to maintain the status quo. Nick's 'problems' are all about him losing his balance.

Over the course of the novel, Nick plays tricks on people, shoots Rose's husband Tom, manipulates Rose into killing Myra, helps save the 'coloured town' from a fire, shoots two pimps for being disrespectful, slyly tricks Ken into boasting that he killed the pimps and shoots an old black man he had earlier saved from a beating. For every positive act, there is a negative one. By trying to counterbalance his external actions, which are becoming increasingly violent, we are being shown the battle within Nick Corey's mind. His escalating madness, his lack of 'restraint' are reminiscent of Kurtz in *Heart Of Darkness*.

Nick fancies himself as some sort of Messiah/Devil figure who exposes the hypocrisy around him. He says to Rose, "It's what I'm supposed to do, you know, to punish the heck out of people for bein' people. To coax them into revealin' theirselves, an' then kick the crap out of 'em." As Robert Polito points out in his Thompson biography, *Savage Art*, Nick Corey's split personality is somewhat similar to the voices Theodore Wieland hears in *Wieland* (1798) by Gothic writer Charles Brockden Brown.

At the end, there is no resolution. We do not know whether Nick or Ken will hang. It does not seem to matter. All Nick knows is that he still has his 'problems' and they have not left him. He does not know what to do. This lack of closure is important because Nick remains enigmatic (and therefore more powerful) and we are forced to think about the content of Thompson's writing. This is in direct contrast to Thompson's first great novel *The Killer Inside Me* (1952), which features easygoing but psychotic Deputy Lou Ford who ends up killing a lot of people before getting his come-uppance. This neat ending allows the audience to sleep safely, secure in the knowledge that evil will never visit their breakfast table.

The root idea for these sadistic cops came from Thompson's own father (an unreliable sheriff who embezzled) and from a meeting with a cop who implied that he could kill the young Thompson without getting caught. The cop told Thompson (as recounted in the autobiographical *Bad Boy* (1953)), "There ain't no way of telling what a man is by looking at him. There ain't no way of knowing what he'll do if he has a chance."

Jim Thompson's life began on September 27 1906 in Anadarko, Oklahoma. It was a life of boon or bust depending on how much money his father had won/stole/made or lost/spent/borrowed. It was a life (like his novels) which revolved around Texas, Oklahoma and Nebraska. When he was old enough, he worked to support his family - as a bellboy, he pimped, acquired liquor and dealt drugs for guests, thus associating with hardened criminals. He acquired a lifelong addiction to alcohol and cigarettes. He worked the Texas oil fields, drifted as a hobo, became a salesman. He wrote for magazines and newspapers, political speeches, plays. There was no job upon which Thompson could rest, his penchant for alcohol securing a reputation for unreliability.

After a couple of unsuccessful hardbacks (*Now And On Earth* (1942) and *Heed The Thunder* (1946)), Thompson hit pay dirt with 750,000 sales of *Nothing More Than Murder* (1949). As a result he became associated with Lion Books, under the editorship of Arnold Hano, a small paperback publisher who specialised in Noir Fiction. Thompson wrote a phenomenal 12 books in 19 months, all but one for Lion, including *The Killer Inside Me* (1952), *Savage Night* (1953, narrated by a tiny, consumptive hit man), *The Criminal* (1953, the effect of a schoolgirl rape/murder with multiple points of view) and *A Hell Of A Woman* (1954, a salesman in lust).

Thompson worked on the film script for *The Killing* (1956, directed by Stanley Kubrick) and finished a few more great novels (*The Getaway* (1959), *The Grifters* (1963), *Pop 1280* (1964)) before the booze took his health away. He also seemed to have lost his heart for writing. The years, like his finances, ebbed and flowed. When he died on April 7 1977, not one of his books was in print.

Then Maxim Jakubowski's Black Box Thriller series introduced Thompson to a new UK audience in 1983. Barry Gifford's Black Lizard series did a similar job for Americans the following year. American films followed 6 years later, and continue to be made. Robert Polito's award-winning biography of Jim Thompson, *Savage Art*, has established this laconic master of apocalyptic psychology as a literary force in American letters. He is now the Noir Fiction plumb line by which all other Noir writers are to be measured.

He ain't dead yet!

David Karp: The Tiger Was Loose Again In The Land

It is very probable that David Karp did not think much of his early novels because they were written very quickly for a small paperback publisher. This is a pity because, as good as his later 'serious' novels are, these formative/ primitive novels have a power and ferocity the later ones lack. What they all have in common is their sense of moral outrage. "If there is such a thing as a moralist novelist I am probably in that class or genre," Karp wrote in 1972. "I am a didactic writer. My first teacher was Upton Sinclair. I devoured all of his works and learned my liberalism from this impassioned teacher. Poverty was given to me by the world into which I was born. I was poor, I was ambitious, I was filled with outrage against injustice and yet I inherited from my mother, I guess, a pragmatism which I have never forgotten."

His stories have ironic endings, where the hunter becomes the hunted, people are caught in their own traps, the characters' strengths are their own undoing. For example, his first novel, *The Big Feeling* (1952 and as *The Gentle Thief* by Wallace Ware, c1967) is about thief Frank Ames who is on trial. His insanity plea may not succeed because of his insanity. On the other hand, *Cry, Flesh* (1952, and as *The Girl On Crown Street* by Wallace Ware, 1967) is about Rose Genovese, who performs a mercy killing. When police detective Cheval investigates the death he falls in love with Rose, and then finds out that she is a murderer. He understands why she killed, so he kills her out of compassion so that she will not suffer the consequences of her actions. Ironically, Cheval is then saved from paying for his murder because his superiors feel the same way as him about mercy killing. The story highlights the double standards of society.

In *The Brotherhood Of Velvet* (1953), James Watterson begins the novel with a family and a job with The Organisation, but The Organisation soon takes both from him. He was once comfortable within the womb of The Organisation, but when the company turns against him, his perception of the world changes. This is Karp's design - to change the perception of the reader by showing his characters change. All of Karp's books are about the individual in society, something Karp passionately believes in.

The individuals Karp chooses as his central characters are outsiders. Thieves, gangsters, amoral company men. His message seems to be: if the evil and obnoxious inhabitants of society can change, then so can we.

Probably Karp's best book from this period is *Hardman* (1952, and as by Wallace Ware, c1967). The back cover reads: 'Spawned on street, bred on gutter, he knew only the law of the whip and the fist. "Crush," he said, was the best word he knew. It was better, he said, to break a man's face with a pistol butt than to knock him out with one punch. And far better, he thought, to claw at a woman's throat with his hands than to kiss her or fondle her.' *Hardman* is about a juvenile delinquent by the name of Jack Hardman, who is a charismatic member of his community. He is brutal, sadistic, uncompromising and worst of all, he is articulate. Whatever the police, the youth workers and the politicians say, Hardman has a convincing answer. When he comes before Judge Olney, the Judge believes that all of Hardman's problems are a result of his environment. He sees Hardman's obvious intelligence and decides it can be harnessed for good instead of evil. The Judge takes Hardman under his wing, and gets him to write down his thoughts and feelings. The result is a blistering series of best-selling books, and a new enfant terrible on the writing scene. He is obnoxious, rude and, of course, made for the media.

Hardman seems to be a comment on both the criminal-turned-writer phenomenon (for example, Caryl Chessman), and crime writers like Mickey Spillane whose writing contains many sadistic scenes. And what happens to Hardman as he acquires money, women, status, and his brutal books continue to be successful? Does he change because of his changed environment? No. It is his nature to be brutal, sadistic, amoral. In fact, rather than change, his work incites people to violence. He is changing society for the worse.

As far as Karp's success goes, he broke into literary circles with *One* (1953 and as *Escape To Nowhere*, 1955), a story of the very near future, where a college professor tries to express himself, only to find the state will not allow it. It is a future where all traces of individuality have been stamped out. The book won him much praise in American and the UK - *One* was produced twice on US television, in 1955 and 1957, and was filmed in the UK in 1956.

Both *The Brotherhood Of Velvet* and *One* are about people who find out that the society they live in is not formed in their best interests. Of course, Karp is referring to our society. He believed that since a writer cannot rely on society, he must maintain his independence and be self-reliant. "A writer's first responsibility is to survive and to be self-sufficient. I don't think a writer is entitled to be a mendicant on the grounds that his art prevents him from being self-supporting. Nor do I think that he should become a freak to exploit his position. A writer has the right to do his work and if it gains acceptance to be modestly grateful and if it is rejected to be immodestly contemptuous but to go on."

David Karp was born May 5 1922 in New York City, where he grew up. Writing was a passion, and he had a book of verse *The Voice Of The Four Freedoms* privately printed in 1942. He served with the 81st Infantry Division in the Philippines and Japan from 1942 to 1946, and married Lillian Klass on Christmas Day 1944. Upon his return, Karp became a freelance radio writer, writing dozens of plays throughout the 1940s and 1950s. He sometimes found it difficult to find work, so he began writing novels to supplement his income. After the break-through success of *One* in 1953, he soon found it easier to get work in television, giving him two careers.

Karp continued writing novels for the next 10 years: *Platoon* as by Adam Singer (1953); *The Charka Memorial* as by Wallace Ware (1954); *The Day Of The Monkey* (1955); *All Honorable Men* (1956); *Leave Me Alone* (1957); *Enter Sleeping* (1960 and as *The Sleepwalkers*, 1960); and *The Last Believers* (1964). As you read, you can discern that there is an intelligence governing the work. And more, it is an uncompromising voice we are listening to. "I will not compromise to be successful, I will not kiss asses to be accepted and I will not give up being a writer because I am ignored. I have written many things - many of them (too many of them) to maintain myself and my family and to maintain my pride in being self-sufficient."

Eventually Karp found regular work during the late 1950s and early 1960s, the so-called Golden Age of television, when his contemporaries were writers like Paddy Chayevsky, Reginald Rose and Rod Serling. He wrote episodes of serials like *The Defenders*, *The Untouchables* and *I Spy* as well as many one-off plays. One play warned of the dangerous power of political bosses (*The Big Vote*). Another told the story of the assassination of Archduke Franz Ferdinand of Austria-Hungary (*The End Of A World*). An episode from John F Kennedy's book *Profiles In Courage* was turned in a play about a senator who held out against the impeachment of President Andrew Johnson. In *The Plot To Kill Stalin*, Karp named several top Soviet leaders as conspirators.

By this time, Karp did not have to worry too much about his scripts being accepted - many of them won awards and nominations. So, towards the end of the 1960s, he wrote some screenplays (*Sol Madrid* (1967), *Ché!* (1968)) and moved into TV and film production, which is where the real power is in the industry. He wrote the television movies *The Brotherhood Of The Bell* and *The Family Rico*, and the TV series *Hawkins On Murder* which starred James Stewart.

After a lifetime of writing, he finally put down his pen on September 11 1999, dying from emphysema brought on by bladder cancer. "People who wait for great moments to make their mark miss the point. Life is made up of thousands upon thousands of tiny marks. Like a sculptor who works in marble - you make your life in flakes and bits and chips and the scourings of marble dust. In the end you have created an image of yourself."

David Goodis: It Was The Very Substance Of Hope

Some years ago, I travelled many miles, queued for hours, suffered vast numbers of people and excessive heat to stand in front of some paintings by Edvard Munch. I was fascinated by the way Munch arranged these disproportionate, lob-sided pictures, by the way he filled them with thin, dejected people, and by the vast areas of blackness surrounding them. It was a dark world, and one with which Munch was obsessed. He drew variations of the same images over and over again. It is this repetitive obsession with despairing images that reminds me of the 'no-hope' novels of David Goodis.

David Goodis (1917-1967) was the bleakest of the Noir Fiction writers. His novels are depressing and, mostly, predictable. Each of them has a once-artistic man drowning his sorrows in a seedy bar, trying to forget the dirty, grotesquely fat woman he hates but is, strangely, sexually attracted to. To save himself, he fixates on a clean, pure, thin, idealised woman. She is his better nature, and represents escape from despair, guilt and self-pity. But all his attempts to hang on to his hope fail. Eventually, he knows that he is doomed, that he cannot escape the fat woman, and that he will die. If he doesn't die by the end of the book, you know he'll have a miserable drunken existence until he does.

Take, for example, *Cassidy's Girl* (1951). It is the story of Philadelphian James Cassidy. He used to be an achiever - college footballer, war hero, a highly-paid airline pilot - then a tragic accident in which 70 people died ruined his career. He was blamed for the crash - no-one believed his co-pilot caused it. Cassidy turned to drink, ended up at the waterfront, among the lowest of the low, at Lundy's Place, where he met and married Mildred. He has an animalistic, antagonistic love-hate relationship with her which is 'a form of degradation.' Cassidy may not be able to control his drinking, or his actions, but at least he can control a bus. When he drives he 'felt as though he belonged to the world.' His route is between Philadelphia and Easton, through the countryside which is 'the very substance of hope.'

When Cassidy and Mildred have a big fight and split, Mildred goes off with corpulent salesman Haney Kendrick, whilst Cassidy shacks up with alcoholic Doris (whose one true love is the drink). But Mildred cannot let go of Cassidy - she hits him, then torments him with her curvaceous, voluptuous body. On the bus Haney, sitting behind Cassidy and drinking heavily, says that the only way Mildred will stop harassing Cassidy (and concentrate on Haney) is if Cassidy crawls back to her on his belly. Haney offers to pay Cassidy to do this. Cassidy refuses. Haney, drunk, slips, knocks out Cassidy. The bus crashes, in the countryside, goes up in flames, kills the passengers. Half conscious, Cassidy feels Haney pouring alcohol down his throat. The police arrive and arrest Cassidy. Hope has no substance any more.

Cassidy escapes from the police, goes on the run and is about to get away by boat but is physically and psychologically dragged back to Mildred and all the other losers at Lundy's Place. Eventually he realises that 'his pity for Doris had been the reflection of pity that he felt for himself. His need for Doris had been the need to find something worthwhile and gallant within himself.' At one stage, his friend Shealy says to Cassidy, "Just wake up every morning and whatever happens, let it happen. Because no matter what you do, it'll happen anyway. So ride with it. Just let it take you." "Down," says Cassidy. Down into the gutter. Slide all the way down. It's easy. No effort involved.

By the end of the book, Cassidy has drowned in his bottle of self-pity, deluded himself into believing that he deserves everything that has happened to him, and calls himself a hypocrite. "There's nothing lower than a hypocrite." In the end, the novel ends on a false high note (like many Goodis novels), because Haney is found out, and Cassidy returns to Mildred. We know they are all doomed, of course.

Born in Philadelphia on March 2 1917, David Goodis studied journalism, worked in an advertising agency and published his first novel *Retreat From Oblivion* in 1939. This literary novel did not meet with success, so Goodis went to New York and launched himself into a pulp & radio writing career where he learnt how to tell a story that people want to follow. He hit the big time with *Dark Passage* (1946), about a man escaping from prison to prove himself innocent and, at the end, continuing to be a fugitive from justice. It became a best-seller, and sold to the movies, turning into a Humphrey Bogart/Lauren Bacall film in 1947. His next novel, *Nightfall* (1947), another man on the run story, was also excellent. Goodis got a gig as a Hollywood screenwriter. Then something went wrong.

Goodis had married Elaine in 1942. He was obsessed by her. She tormented him. She left after a year and Goodis could not forget her. He pursued her, without success. She became the central wicked woman of *Behold This Woman* (1947). She was the erotic obsession which haunted his books. His commercial writing suffered, lost direction. In 1950, Goodis returned to Philadelphia to live with his parents, and began writing the kind of lowlife, obsessional novels for which he has been justifiably praised. The best of these are *The Burglar* (1953), *The Moon In The Gutter* (1953), *Black Friday* (1954), *Street Of No Return* (1954) and *Down There* (1956, as *Shoot The Piano Player* (1960), famously filmed by François Truffaut in 1960).

Goodis was obsessed with big, black, abusive women. He often drank himself into oblivion. When he worked in Hollywood, he lived on a sofa which he rented for $4 a month. He wore the same suits until threadbare, then dyed them blue. This seedy existence is the substance of his work. When reading the novels, one is reminded of the Parisian lowlife in the novels of Francis Carco (*Perversity*), and the oppressive, violent atmosphere of Hubert Selby Jr's *Last Exit To Brooklyn*. Goodis' work is very well respected in France (where there have been at least 8 film adaptations), and has gained an increasing number of admirers in America, including Paul Thomas Anderson, director of the films *Boogie Nights* and *Magnolia*, who recently cited David Goodis as a literary influence (along with J D Salinger and David Mamet).

The Goodis central character is hell-bent on self-destruction. There is no redemption for his sins. The squalid environment reflects his interior self-hate and confusion. He tries to change himself (his face in *Dark Passage*), or job (*Down There*, *Cassidy's Girl*) or environment (to escape the prison). He wants to wipe the slate clean, start again, to renew, to forget, only to find that he cannot change himself. In *The Burglar*, Goodis wrote, 'Every animal, including the human being, is a criminal, and every move in life is part of the vast process of crime.' (It is a thought reminiscent of Joseph Conrad.) Everybody is guilty, has been caught, and is imprisoned. The point of each novel is to show the central character being stripped of all hope of escape or happiness, so that he learns to accept his pitiless existence.

Yet, in contrast, Goodis the man was said to be a jovial character, who was more interested in the mechanics of writing than the substance. The single-minded intensity of his work reveals the truth. Goodis was like James Cassidy, driving his bus with outward control waiting for the inner catastrophe. Goodis' novels are that inner catastrophe made flesh.

In Philadelphia, despite his avuncular behaviour, the thread which held Goodis' life together began to unravel. He made arrangements for the care of his schizophrenic brother. He helped look after his father, who died in 1963. In 1965, he brought a lawsuit against the producers of the hit TV show *The Fugitive*, believing they had based it on *Dark Passage*. His mother died in 1966. He admitted himself into a psychiatric hospital the same year and died on January 7 1967. He was only 49.

Apathy (1960-1978)

With the austerity of the 1950s making way for the prosperity of the 1960s, the comfortable masses began to clasp middle-class values to their bosom. Generally, they were apathetic about the problems of others because they were comfortable in their own houses.

Now killers were a 'problem' and we had to find out why they killed. Was it the low-life society they were brought up in? Or was it their nature to kill? These were the main concerns of the crime novels of Colin Wilson. They are about intelligent men who rip and defile people for reasons which are beyond the understanding of society. Their lucid ideas are drowned by their repulsive actions. Beginning with *Ritual In The Dark* (1960), the focus of Wilson's books are the killers and their hunters. Both are treated as artists, as intellectuals. The victims are forgotten. These novels are at least 20 years ahead of their time in terms of psychology, but the characters do not engage the emotions. Essentially, these stories are a way for Wilson to explain his philosophy of life (brilliantly explained in his non-fiction work *The Outsider*). Consequently, the quest for truth is not the truth society is looking for, but the truth an individual finds.

Another 'cold' writer who addressed these issues was Patricia Highsmith. Her first novel *Strangers On A Train* (1950) uses the idea of two people switching murders. Since the police base their theories on motive, a crime without proven motive cannot be solved. She hit upon an even more compelling idea in her masterpiece *The Talented Mr Ripley* (1955). In this story, Tom Ripley is a grasping young man, just the wrong side of the law, always looking for 'opportunities.' When he is sent to Europe to persuade Dickie Greenleaf to return to America, Tom ends up liking Dickie. There are homosexual undertones to the relationship. When Dickie realises this, he backs away and wants to end the friendship. Tom is not happy about this: 'He had offered Dickie friendship, companionship, and respect, everything he had to offer, and Dickie had replied with ingratitude and now hostility.' Tom decides to kill Dickie, and then has the idea of taking Dickie's place. Tom realises he admires Dickie's lifestyle not his personality. Coldly, Tom plans the murder. He executes it clumsily, but gets away with it. The opening sentence of the novel describes Tom looking over his shoulder, expecting the police to be there. At the end, having been given Dickie's inheritance (as indicated in the will Tom forged), he is looking forward to a splendid life in Europe, but still expecting policemen to be waiting for him. Nothing has really changed in his life. In Highsmith's work, there is no obvious moral judgement - you have to work that out for yourself. Some readers would say that Tom was perfectly justified in killing people because they were so horrible, or stupid, or philistines or whatever. It is an amazing achievement that Highsmith has persuaded so many readers to take Ripley's point of view. Tom went on to feature in 4 further novels over the next 40 years.

Patricia Highsmith wrote many novels delving into the psychology of ordinary people, proving that they were in fact quite extraordinary. Patrick Hamilton also took upper middle-class people and showed the hypocrisy of their lives. In 1951, he began a quartet of novels about Mr Ernest Ralph Gorse, a character based on the English murderer Neville George Clevely Heath, with *The West Pier*. It was followed by *Mr Stimpson And Mr Gorse* (1953) and *Unknown Assailant* (1955). The fourth book was never completed - Hamilton's drinking and emotional problems over the last years of his life interfered with his muse. Over the course of the novels, Gorse uses his charmingly smooth veneer to enter the lives of women to woo them, seduce them and then take their money. Gorse succeeds in both emotionally and financially destroying his victims. To a certain extent, he prefigures Tom Ripley.

Like Highsmith, Hamilton was interested in aberrant personalities. His most famous dip into this mutant gene pool is the play *Rope* (1929), which was based on the notorious Leopold-Loeb case. It is the story of two students who decide to kill someone for the intellectual challenge of it, to prove their superiority over the rest of the human race. (The homosexual aspect, the duality, the single room, the men believing themselves cleverer than others, all point to immobilised men, no?) Even better is Hamilton's novel *Hangover Square* (1941). It is the story of George Harvey Bone, a man in two minds - a schizophrenic. At the beginning, he knows he must kill Netta and Peter and then go to Maidenhead. There is a click in his head and he becomes the other George. He is detached from the world. He knows he is sick, and what he wants to do is wrong, but he must do it. He drinks heavily, to soothe his unease, and suffers for it (which his friend Mickey calls 'a little stroll around Hangover Square.') George's very English voice gives the whole novel a feeling of black comedy. Towards the end, his head clicks, and he asks himself why Netta and Peter are not dead - they should have been dead weeks ago! He telephones them, just to make sure they are not dead, and then gets down to business.

There are two other writers from this period who are of great interest. Charles Willeford is now well known because of his excellent Hoke Moseley series, but many of his earlier novels are also worth examining because they deal with the existential quality of men in the later half of the 20th Century. Equally chilling is the work of the largely-ignored Shane Stevens whose moral and amoral characters are equally capable of horrific acts of violence.

Charles Willeford: Nothing Exists

At the beginning of *Miami Blues* (1984), a Hare Krishna goes up to Junior Frenger and asks for a contribution. Junior grabs his middle finger, bends it back, snaps it and leaves the guy writhing on the floor in tremendous pain. The Hare Krishna dies of shock.

This off-hand violence reverberates throughout Willeford's novels. It is as if we all lead fragile lives which can be transformed or destroyed by small acts. We hear the wind whistling through our houses, maybe even slamming our doors, but we cannot imagine such a puny thing destroying everything we possess. Charles Willeford lived with that possibility throughout his later life - he lived in hurricane central, Miami. This fragile fist is never mentioned in his novels, but we know it is there, waiting.

Whilst reading *Something About A Soldier* (1986), Willeford's memoirs of life in the Army pre-World War Two, it becomes obvious that Willeford's ideas about men were formed there. The anecdotes and observations describe the things men do to occupy their time whilst stationed in the Philippines. This mainly means sexual encounters with the local prostitutes and violent acts upon those weaker than themselves. There is no right or wrong, no morality, no fairness. One story tells of a respected Army doctor who requisitioned unclaimed Filipino corpses for educational skeletons. In fact, in his spare time he used leg bones and a skull to fashion an ashtray, and tanned skin (with hair intact) to make a watch strap.

In an interview, Willeford commented, "A good half of the men you deal with in the Army are psychopaths. There's a pretty hefty overlap between the military population and the prison population, so I knew plenty of guys like Junior in *Miami Blues* and Troy in *Sideswipe*." During World War Two, Willeford was a tank commander with the 10th Armoured Division and saw action in the Battle Of The Bulge. "Like, some of these other Tankers I knew used to swap bottles of liquor with infantrymen in exchange for prisoners, and then just shoot 'em for fun. I used to say, 'Goddamn it, will you stop shooting those prisoners!' And they would just shrug and say, 'Hell, they'd shoot us if they caught us!' Which was true, they used to shoot any Tankers they captured. So that sort of behaviour became normal to them, and I used to wonder, 'What's gonna happen to these guys when they go back into civilian life? How are they gonna act?' You can't just turn it off and go to work in a 7-11. If you're good with weapons or something in the Army, you're naturally gonna do something with weapons when you get out, whether it's being a cop or a criminal. These guys learned to do all sorts of things in the Army that just weren't considered normal by civilian standards."

Men are the subject of Willeford's books, not women. The women in the books are generally sensible, solid citizens, their choices based on good emotional reasoning. Women in his books will love bad men but will not carry out bad acts themselves.

Willeford does not judge his characters and does not tell you how to think. He shows you what kind of people they are, and the results of their actions.

Willeford once commented that the prominent theme of most post-war American fiction is of the reluctant lover - the story of a man who wants to fuck a gal silly but does not want to commit to a lasting relationship. If he does not want a relationship, what does he want? Willeford answers...

His theme is the sexually obsessive man, the competitive man, the intelligent man who must prove himself better than others. This man cannot live quietly with another human being. He must control, defeat, destroy the other. This done, the man must move on to the next challenger.

Man was born good and the only choice he can make is to do bad. Too many men make that choice.

Born January 2 1919 in Little Rock, Arkansas, Charles Ray Willeford III was orphaned at the age of 8. He lived with his grandmother in Los Angeles until he was 12. Realising she could not support him in Depression-era America, Charles hit the hobo trail. He later documented this period of his life in *I Was Looking For A Street* (1986).

At 16 he dropped out of Junior High school, lied about his age and joined the Army Air Corps. Initially stationed in the Philippines pre-World War Two, he got bored with that and moved on to showing horses for the cavalry before becoming a highly decorated (Silver Star, Bronze Star, Purple Heart, Luxembourg Croix de Guerre) tank commander. He had the scars to go with the medals: shrapnel wounds to his face and backside. He never talked about his war experiences. After the war, with no opportunity for a civilian job, he stayed on in the Army for another 10 years.

Willeford had always harboured dreams of becoming a poet - his first poem *Dansant* was about ants biting him. He appeared in *The Outcast Poets* (1947), and had his own book *Proletarian Laughter* (1948) published, before being posted to Tokyo in 1948. With access to a radio station and lots of free time, he began writing a soap opera serial *The Saga Of Mary Miller*. Then he moved to Hamilton Air Force Base, California, in 1949. Goaded into writing a novel by his bunkmates, over the summer Willeford wrote in a San Francisco apartment during his weekend leave. He hawked the manuscript around the leading paperback publishers. Eventually, making his way down the literary food chain, Willeford got an acceptance letter from Beacon and published *High Priest Of California* in 1953. He stayed with Beacon, publishing *Pick Up* (1955, a man on the way down into drunkenness and alienation from society, reads more like Harry Crews or Charles Bukowski), *Wild Wives* (1956, a slick private eye novel), *Honey Gal* (1958 and as *The Black Mass Of Brother Springer*, 1989, a comedic existentialist novel), and *Lust Is A Woman* (1958 and as *Sex Is A Woman*, as good as it sounds). Willeford then moved on to publishers Newsstand Library, to whom he delivered *The Woman Chaser* (1960, a novel about a grifter/film director), *Understudy For Love* (1961, with Willeford forced to insert sex scenes), and *No Experience Necessary* (1962, where an editor rewrote large chunks).

Then Willeford decided to write a novel based on the voyages of Ulysses, but set in the American Deep South. The book was the masterful *Cockfighter* (1962, reprinted in an expanded form in 1972), which is narrated by Frank Mansfield, who is silent throughout the book. This is about Frank's single-minded obsession to become Cockfighter of the Year. The opening quote by Ezra Pound is, 'What matters is not the idea a man holds, but the depth at which he holds it.' This pretty much sums up the book.

Willeford retired from the Army in 1956. He had many jobs, studied Art, got his English BA in 1962, and was the Associate Editor of *Alfred Hitchcock's Murder Magazine* in 1964. Willeford then taught humanities at the University of Miami for 3 years, then English and philosophy at Miami-Dade Junior College for 18 years, becoming Associate Professor. He wrote regular columns for *Village Voice* and *Mystery Scene*, and was crime fiction reviewer for the *Miami Herald*.

After the existential western *The Hombre From Sonora* (1971 as by Will Charles), and the fictional retelling of the Son of Sam murders in *Off The Wall* (1980), Willeford began to receive both critical and financial recognition when he started a series of books starring old worn-out cop Hoke Moseley. The first, *Miami Blues* (St Martin's Press, 1984), is an ode to the greed generation. When Junior Frenger blows into town like some dark wind, he hooks up with prostitute Susan and they begin to act like a family, consuming everything they can find. Junior seizes each opportunity to live life to the full, even if it means taking the lives of others. He preys on the weak, which include Hoke - Junior steals Hoke's gun and throws away his false teeth. In *New Hope For The Dead* (1985), Hoke is hoping to retire and is given the old case files to reinvestigate. In this book, it is Hoke who begins to acquire a new family, balancing his female assistant and his 2 teenage daughters. *Sideswipe* (1987) delves deeper into Willeford's ideas about the Immobilised Man - in the first half Hoke, suffering from combat fatigue, is paralysed. Meanwhile, happy-go-lucky psychopath Troy Loudon is assembling crims for a liquor store heist. Finally, in *The Way We Die Now* (1988), Hoke kills all the villains in the first quarter and spends the rest of the book wondering whether the ex-con he once put away, and who is now living opposite, has really gone straight.

As great as these novels are, *The Burnt Orange Heresy* (1971) is probably Willeford's best novel. It is about up-and-coming art critic Jamie Figueras who wants to become as immortal as the artists he promotes through his writing. This is the story about the commerce of art criticism, dealers and collectors, and the way they exploit the artist. Figueras hunts down the world's greatest artist, a 90-year-old man whose work has only been seen by 4 art critics. James wants to be the fifth, by fair means or foul. On another level, this reads like a critique of academic life. Figueras is the archetypal amoral Willeford character, only looking out for himself, ignoring the needs of others. (This selfishness harks back to Camus' *The Outsider*. We follow Meursault, but what happened to the Arab girlfriend? And what about the death of her brother?) Figueras is a man with no restraint, or morals. He is a hollow man, living in a hollow world, where nothing exists.

After receiving the critical recognition he deserved with the Hoke Moseley series, Willeford died in 1988, in Miami. His books and writings continue to be published.

Shane Stevens: A Man Got No Time To Be Sorry

Shocked. Horrified. Terrified. These are the words most used by people who read the novels of Shane Stevens. He portrays worlds which exist side by side with our own - worlds we hope we never have to encounter. He describes the thoughts of people who consider murder a viable option in their decision-making processes. Their thinking is perfectly logical. The world is perfectly horrible. Some of the people in it are not much better.

'One thing about living here in Harlem you know it cant get no worse.' So begins *Go Down Dead* (1967). This is the story of 8 days in the life of 16-

year-old Adam Clayton Henry, an intelligent juvenile delinquent. He is called King Henry and is leader of The Playboys. All they have to live for is the respect that their tawdry exploits bring to them. Mainly, they spend their time taunting and fighting rival gang The Tigers - the fights/rumbles result in mutilation and death.

King knows that it is all for nothing, yet still he persists in leading The Playboys and putting on the pretence that he is one hard mother. He spends the whole book trying to buy firesticks (guns) so that they become top gang. To get the money to buy the guns, King stars in a stag movie and deals in drugs. After a week of this, The Playboys and The Tigers get to fight.

The reason for it all? Stevens presents it as the only way for The Playboys to protect Harlem, to stop it becoming an even worse place to live. King Henry is disgusted by the things he has to do to protect the place he lives in. So, perhaps, it is not just an accurate portrayal of Harlem gang life, but also an allegory for the evils that man has to do to maintain his environment. There is no sense that things will change in Harlem.

Everybody from outside (the youth workers, the teachers) is fooled and exploited to the full. The school is a centre for criminal activities. The white world ignores what is happening in Harlem - they turn a blind eye. King Henry does not blame them, or care. He is a realist, and knows that he has to deal with the cards he is dealt, no matter how bad the hand. He can see the wasted lives around him. He can see the futility of trying to change the world. Each new generation will repeat the mistakes of the previous one.

Told in the voice of King Henry, Stevens began writing *Go Down Dead* in Harlem in 1959, and then added to the manuscript as he travelled to San Francisco, Mexico, South America, Europe, Asia and Africa. He finished it, "in a burst of love in mother New York, 1966." After the manuscript "was accepted for publication by the first publisher to see it, then rejected because of racial antagonism," it was rejected by Morrow, who then accepted it for publication after getting opinions from top literary critics.

Go Down Dead is the first in a loose trilogy of books. *Way Uptown In Another World* (1971) is a satiric odyssey about exploitation and reads like a black version of *Midnight Cowboy* or even *Candide*. The third book, *Rat Pack* (1974), is set over one night. A small group of black kids roam Central Park and the surrounding environs, wreaking havoc wherever they pause. Over their journey, we see how the dynamics of the group expose the tensions inherent in black society at that time. At the same time, this shows how black anger and frustration can explode outside of the ghetto and into the white neighbourhoods. Perhaps now the whites will take notice of the exploited people in their society? Or perhaps not.

Very little is known about Shane Stevens the person, mainly because he wants it that way. It is known that he was born in New York City on October 8 1941, that he grew up in Hell's Kitchen, later Harlem. Stevens was 14 when he decided he wanted to be a novelist, after reading Ernest Hemingway, Nathanael West and F Scott Fitzgerald. "I liked the way books could take me to far-off places, the way they could put me with people who were doing wild and wonderful things." He got his Masters Degree from Columbia University in 1961. After that, you could write his biography on the back of an envelope, a very small envelope. "I am very secretive," he said. "I am a novelist: that's my punishment for living... I am a writer always, now and forever; nothing I would do could shatter the significance of that. Whatever I have done in my life, I have done with that in mind. The details are of no consequence.... I never give interviews, stay in shadow, travel by night. I don't associate with writers, don't do book reviews, don't play politics or give advice. I try not to hurt anyone. I go where I want and write what I want."

Stevens shifted his attention to organised crime with *Dead City* (1973). It follows the fall and rise of two foot soldiers in The Syndicate. Charley Flowers is an old-timer who was doing great until he screwed up. Demoted to muscle jobs, he works for Joe Zucco in Jersey City. New blood Harry Strega got educated in Vietnam, and is trying to make his way up the ladder. He is prepared to do anything to get himself noticed by his bosses. We follow their paths separately, as they try to hit the big time - to be considered so good that they can become contract killers. This is the best that they can hope for - to get the respect that being a contract killer demands. Each day, they are given new challenges by their bosses. Each day, they have to prove their loyalty with increasingly brutal tasks. Only the hardest, most sadistic, amoral soldiers can hope to get noticed, and perhaps move up the chain. They do things which go against every moral fibre in my being, yet still I must read on.

But if you want to see into the mind of a modern killer, then you should meet Thomas Bishop in *By Reason Of Insanity* (1979). He escapes from an insane asylum and, aged only 25, sets out to become the world's best multiple murderer. Again, like in other Stevens novels, he has a career path, he is meticulous, he is intelligent, he is completely aware of his actions and is utterly amoral. *By Reason Of Insanity* is easily the best psycho-killer novel ever written and also one of the earliest, coming before Thomas Harris (*Red Dragon*), James Ellroy (*Killer On The Road/Silent Terror*) and Bradley Denton (*Blackburn*).

Thomas Bishop tells us the problems he has to overcome to ensure a good clean kill. Each kill must be different so that he does not have a recognisable MO - his murders cannot then be identified as a sequence. He murders irregularly, and without a geographical pattern for the same reason. As Bishop tells us his story, he also tells us his family history - about how his father was the Red Light Bandit aka Caryl Chessman. Bishop wants to become part of the mythology that surrounds famous murders and murderers. Only to become this famous, he must first remain anonymous. Finally, Bishop decides to do something which has never been done before, which will win him eternal fame and notoriety.

In all of these novels, the police exist only as occasional intrusions - they have no power in the world of the central characters. Stevens changed the emphasis in his next book by having a French police detective hunt for a Nazi who was presumed long dead. *The Anvil Chorus* (1985) reads very much like other books of its ilk (*The Ipcress File*, *The Boys From Brazil*) and is an enjoyable romp, but it does not have the same intimate epic/gut-wrenching feeling of Stevens' earlier novels. Stevens then issued two Private Eye novels under the pseudonym J W Rider. *Jersey Tomatoes* (1986), winner of the Shamus Award for the best first Private Eye novel, was followed in quick succession by *Hot Tickets* (1987). Although Stevens is as readable as ever, and the language is accurate, his books read more like he were copying what has gone before rather than ploughing new ground.

Hollywood beckoned in the mid-1970s. Stevens wrote screenplays for *The Me Nobody Knows* and *By Reason Of Insanity*, and seems to have stayed there ever since. There has been talk of him writing screenplays, but he has never been credited as Shane Stevens. It may have been 15 years since Shane Stevens last appeared in print under his own name, but his legend continues to grow regardless.

Amorality (1979-Present)

When Shane Stevens published *By Reason Of Insanity* in 1979, he ushered in the new Noir age of the psychokiller, the amoral mobile man. No longer confined to his room, he could walk, run and jump into your neighbourhood. He was that shadow sitting in the car just down the road. He was that phone call that would ring off just as you picked up the receiver. He was that uneasy feeling you had in the pit of your stomach when the journey home required you to enter shadows. He was the place where nobody could help you. Thomas Harris (*Red Dragon* (1981)), Bret Easton Ellis (*American Psycho* (1991)) and Bradley Denton (*Blackburn* (1993)) have all written psycho-killer novels. The heart of darkness was getting very dark indeed. Welcome to Psychoville.

Other writers had their versions of Noir Fiction. Barry Gifford began like a latter-day B Traven with *Port Tropique* (1980) and then, from 1990 onwards, went wild at heart and weird on top with the Sailor & Lula novels. James Sallis took the life of Lew Griffin, a black private eye, operating in New Orleans and dissected his life into slices of time. Griffin is a debt collector who ends up giving money to people to pay their debts. Lew Griffin is a murderer. He is a lecturer on European literature. He is a novelist. Sallis plays with Griffin's life to such an extent that the narrator (who may or may not be Griffin) becomes unreliable. From book to book, the same events are remembered in different ways. The high point of the series is *Eye Of The Cricket* (1997), which is about fathers & sons losing each other. Sallis said it was, "the single novel in which I think I was able to gather up all the strands and vagaries of the other books, and suffuse the whole with an almost dreamlike poetic intensity." That intensity was achieved at great personal loss to Sallis - his son killed himself as Don Walsh's son kills himself. We cannot escape harsh reality, only learn to deal with it. Edward Bunker does not need to research his books – he has lived them. He lived a life of crime because he had to – once he was in, he had to stay in. This is explained most clearly in his first novel, *No Beast So Fierce* (1972, as *Straight Time*, 1978), which describes how a criminal is trapped by the interdependent nature of the life. His finest novel is *Little Boy Blue* (1981) which follows the tragic story of Bunker's thinly-veiled childhood. Bunker does not pull punches. We finish the book dazed.

Two of the most exciting Noir Fiction writers in recent years are Derek Raymond and James Ellroy. As they write, their stories and subjects evolve. They find out about themselves through their work. Through the exploration of their hearts.

James Ellroy: Love Me Fierce In Danger

From *Brown's Requiem* (1981) to *The Cold Six Thousand* (2000), Ellroy's books are full of swearing, racism, drugs, bodily functions, violence, fluids and sleazeballs. The fuel which keeps Ellroy up nights writing his fever dreams is the unsolved murder of his mother in 1958. His books are full of mother substitutes. It is as though he was trying to deny his mother's reality by treating her as fiction. However, Ellroy showed a greater maturity with his novel *American Tabloid* (1995) and, with the publication of *My Dark Places* (1996), which details Ellroy's search for his mother's murderer, he hopes to acknowledge his mother, to recognise her for the person she really was.

James Ellroy was born March 4 1948 in Good Samaritan Hospital. In 1954, his parents Lee and Jean divorced. Lee drank Alka-Seltzer for his ulcer and chased women. Jean drank Early Times bourbon and chased men. James drank what he was given and did some middle distance running at school. Result: James lived with his mother during the week and his father most weekends.

Jean worked as a nurse at the Packard Bell electronics plant and went out with men on a regular basis. She was always pissed. James preferred his father. When he turned 10, he was given the choice of living with mother or father - he chose his father, his mother slapped him, he called her a drunk and a whore.

Three months later, he arrived back from a weekend with his father to find cops at his mother's house. They told him his mother was dead, a cop gave him some candy, a news photographer snapped him at a neighbour's workbench holding an awl - they didn't use the second picture of him clowning, showing off.

James begged off the funeral. Moved in with father, freelance accountant, womaniser, minor hero in the war, bullshit artist, a history of heart disease. Briefly, Rita Hayworth's business manager in late 1940s. He wondered whether his father was going to be murdered as well. The following year, his father gave him a copy of *The Badge* by Jack Webb, which included a summary of the Black Dahlia case - Elizabeth Short, a starlet tortured and mutilated, found naked and in two halves, reminded James of his mother, neither case solved.

James used to ride over to the spot on Norton Avenue and 39th Street, where the Black Dahlia's body was dumped, to feel her presence. He had nightmares about her, saw her in daylight flashes. Read crime novels from that time on. True crime too. He talked about the Dahlia case with Randy Rice, childhood friend. Kicked out of school for truancy. Years later, he went to Black Dahlia's grave, felt that he knew her, loved her.

Aged 17, James went into the US Army, then his father became gravely ill, so James faked a nervous breakdown, stammered, to get kicked out. His father died. James was virtually penniless and homeless.

1965. Ellroy became a peeper around Hancock Park, breaking and entering, sniffing women's underpants in South Arden. Bought amphetamines from Gene The Short Queen. When no money, Ellroy drank cough syrup, or swallowed cotton wads in nasal inhalers to get high. He spent nights in Robert Burns Park taking speed and masturbating. This was his life for 11 years, drinking, stealing food, drinking, dropping acid, drinking, shoplifting, stealing drink, smoking Maryjane, living on the streets, lifting wallets, sleeping in dumpsters, flophouses. In and out of county jail more than a dozen times. Had odd jobs, once minded till at a porn shop until his hand was found in it.

Ellroy caught pneumonia and was told he had an abscess on a lung. Couple of weeks later was hearing things from the drink. He knew he'd die if he didn't quit the life. Ellroy quit. He joined Alcoholics Anonymous.

Today, Ellroy doesn't drink, doesn't smoke, goes to bed early. He's very neat, meticulous, keeps a neat house, is disciplined. He presently lives with his wife, feminist author and critic, Helen Knode, in Mission Hills, Kansas. Ellroy says that it is "the Hancock Park of the mid-West. I own a house like those, now. The surroundings are restful and physically beautiful and they underscore the silence that I need to work. I abhor outside stimulation."

1977: Ellroy caddying at the Hillcrest and, after punching another caddy, the Bel-Air Country Club for $200-300 a week, whilst living in a $25-a-week room at the Westwood Hotel. He got the idea for a private eye novel in 1978 and began writing *Brown's Requiem* January 26 1979. Published in 1981, it contains all the Ellroy trademarks: corrupt cops; excessive violence; the Black Dahlia case; our hero getting beaten to a pulp; Tijuana; dogs; wine, women & drugs; the unobtainable woman; and the bitter-sweet conclusion. "I wrote that book shortly after I got sober. I hadn't been with a woman for years and years and years. I'd had scant experience with women prior to that and I was looking for THE woman. I wanted a woman, I wanted sex, I wanted all that stuff and I wasn't getting any, and that's what really informs that book."

Ellroy followed it up with *Clandestine* (1982), a thinly veiled, chronologically altered account of his mother's killing. He used many of his father's physical attributes when describing the killer, and doesn't know why he did this. This is Ellroy's first historical novel, set in early 1950s LA, and it introduces us to Dudley Smith, who later played a crucial part in the LA Quartet.

Then there was a trilogy starring contemporary over-the-edge right-wing bastard police detective Lloyd Hopkins who is often more dangerous than the criminals he hunts: *Blood On The Moon* (1984); *Because The Night* (1985); and *Suicide Hill* (1986). His next book, *Silent Terror* (1986, also as *Killer On The Road*), is the first-person narrative of serial killer Martin Michael Plunkett as he travels across America killing all and sundry.

Ellroy got down to serious business with the first novel of his LA Quartet: *The Black Dahlia* (1987). Set against the fictionalised account of the hunt for the true-life murderer of The Black Dahlia in January 1947, this is really the story of two death-obsessed cops, Bucky Bleichert and Lee Blanchard. It was soon followed by *The Big Nowhere* (1988) - moving to 1950, using a red scare commie-bashing investigating team as background, Ellroy shows us Danny Upshaw, ambitious death-obsessed deputy with a string of mutilated victims on his hands, Mal Considine, ambitious DA creep who wants power to get custody of his adopted kid, and Buzz Meeks, loveable ex-cop pimp for Howard Hughes. Death, deceit and double-cross. Lovely.

The third book of the series has become the most widely known because of the recent film: *LA Confidential* (1990). From an enormous cast of characters, about eighty, Ellroy focuses a beady eye on three cops: Trashcan Jack Vincennes (media cop for hire), Ed Exley (overshadowed by his famous father) and Bud White (the toughest of tough LA cops, he's haunted by a wife-beating father). The elements: a Disneyland-like theme park under construction, a series of grisly murders, a cop Christmas party that goes horribly wrong and the cover-up that follows, and Hush-Hush magazine - sleazesheet to the slags with no end of sinuendo. Ellroy delivered an 809-page manuscript which his agent Nat Sobel advised to cut by taking out unnecessary words. Resulted in clipped cadence style which sounds like a rhythmic psycho-beatnik rap. Ellroy took this style to its limit with *White Jazz* (1992). It is told from the point of view of Lieutenant Dave Klein: lawyer, bagman, slum landlord, mob killer... a very bad lieutenant indeed. "*White Jazz* is definitely a one-off. The book is a fever dream - it's a stream of consciousness style -

there are no tricks in it - everything is quite literal but, if you blink, you will miss things. You have to get into the rhythm of Dave Klein's head or you won't get the book at all. There are many people who didn't understand the book. The book did not sell as well as the three previous volumes of the LA Quartet. It was a risk I took - I think the risk is worth it. The important thing with me is always the book, not the sales. I did it for that one book and I returned to a more fully developed style for *American Tabloid*, and I will never go back to *White Jazz* again."

For Ellroy, *White Jazz* was the Noir to end all Noir novels. "When I finished the LA Quartet, I realised that I never wanted to do another novel that could in any way be categorised as a thriller, a mystery or a book based around police work or, specifically police investigations. I realised, what I wanted to do was write a trilogy - three books with 15 years of American history broken down into 5-year increments. I wanted one theme to pervade these works and that is politics as crime and the private nightmare of public policy. The genesis of all this is reading Don DeLillo's novel *Libra*, a brilliantly fictional take on Lee Harvey Oswald and the Kennedy assassination." The first book of the trilogy, *American Tabloid*, is not driven by psycho-sexual plots, but by relationships between men and women. It seems that Ellroy's fiction has begun to mature. To move from loners to relationships. This was confirmed by the second part of the trilogy *The Cold Six Thousand*.

Early in 1994, a newspaper writer in Los Angeles told Ellroy he was going to write a piece about 5 unsolved, uncelebrated St Gabriel Valley homicides and that he was going to review the relevant police files - Ellroy's mother among them. Ellroy decided he had to see this file. "It was just as shocking an experience as you would think it would be. I saw the pictures of my mother nude on the morgue slab. I saw pictures of her dead, a nylon stocking around her neck, where her body had been dumped. And a little click went off in my head, and it meant that this wasn't over. Also, there was a little sub-click that meant 'oh.' And what that 'oh' means is 'You've exploited the similarities between your mother's death and the Black Dahlia murder case for many years, you've exploited your mother's death because it made you a crime writer, and now you have to come back and embrace this woman for the first time, you have to acknowledge her, you have to pay the debt, you have to find out who she is, and to do this you have to find the man who killed her, as unlikely as your success in this endeavour could ever be.'"

With LA County Sheriff's homicide detective Bill Stoner, who became his best friend, Ellroy spent 10 months hunting the man who killed his mother. The book, *My Dark Places*, was Ellroy's autobiography, Bill Stoner's biography and Geneva Hilliker Ellroy's biography. They interviewed many old people, "many of them with faulty memories. They hem and they haw, they digress off the point. It's not linear. It's not like the bullshit homicide investigations your read in my books and the books of crime writers good, bad and indifferent. One thing does not lead to another. It's one dead end after record check after unsatisfying interview after another after another. But facts about my mother and her life are being gleaned en route. Stories and sub-stories are weaving themselves into the tapestry." Ellroy's book was one hell of a tapestry.

"For me, my big thematic journey is 20th Century American history and what I think 20th Century American history is, is the story of bad white men, soldiers of fortune, shakedown artists, extortionists, leg-breakers. The lowest level implementers of public policy. Men who are often toadies of right wing regimes. Men who are racists. Men who are homophobes. These are my guys. These are the guys that I embrace. These are the guys that I empathise with. These are the guys that I love.

"The bottom line is that 20th century American crime fiction is the story of bad white men and I'll go to my grave thinking that."

Derek Raymond:
The Neglected Dead Made Their Decay Known

In the 1960s, as Robin Cook (Derek Raymond's real name), he wrote about wide boy chancers and conmen as heroes, or about seedy Soho pornographers and their friendly priests. Crime was fun in the swinging 1960s, especially since Robin Cook was a criminal and making a good living out of it.

However, years of hard labour in Italian and French vineyards, and a sober face-to-face with reality, resulted in a remarkable series of books where the dead victims had names and the police detective investigating their deaths did not. The Factory novels, as they are known, dance on the edge of the abyss of death, destruction and failure, jump in, wallow in it, and somehow manage to retain their humanity when all about them lose theirs. The heart of darkness beats.

Born June 12 1931 into a well-to-do family. Educated at Eton during and just after World War Two. Walked out when he had enough. "Only man who hated it as much as me was [George] Orwell. Absolutely vile place. Hotbed of vice." Did his national service digging latrines for a tank regiment. Popped off to Spain for a fortnight, ended up there 4 years. The smuggling of cars and tape recorders took place between several countries. Also spent time in America (as a waiter), Italy, Morocco and Turkey. Wrote 9 unpublished novels, the major one being *The Interns*, of which only extracts survive.

Fresh off the boat from New York in 1960, Robin walked into The French House pub, in the heart of London's Soho, and ran into a friend who got him a job managing 5 companies for conman Charles Da Silva. East End thugs, being known to the police, needed fronts, so who better than respectable types like Robin? He sold investments in new houses on the South coast that never got built, then handed over thousands of pounds to his 'fellow busi-nessmen' (The Krays) at the Dorchester or Ritz.

By 1965 he was out of a job and skint. He bumped into another friend at The French House and ended up minding the till at a porn bookshop in St Anne's Court. The sign behind the counter read: 'The following MPs will not be served...' Later minicab driver and abattoir assistant. All these experi-ences ended up in his books written as Robin Cook: *The Crust On Its Uppers* (1962); *Bombe Surprise* (1963); *The Legacy Of The Stiff Upper Lip* (1966); *Public Parts And Private Places* (1967); *A State Of Denmark* (1970); *The Tenants Of Dirt Street* (1971).

When Charles Da Silva received a visit and ended up dead, Robin decided to say goodbye to England for a few years. He spent most of his time in French vineyards during the 1970s and 1980s. Started writing again, this time from the other side of crime, and became a celebrated author in France. (Robin published 2 books in French which have never been translated, *Le Soleil Qui S'éteint* (1983, a so-so spy thriller about an anti-terrorist agency) and *Nightmare In The Street* (1987, "...a failure as a book, and I am far from being to only person to think so.")

The Factory novels were published in English under the pseudonym Derek Raymond so that people were not confused with the medical thriller writer Robin Cook. Factory, is what both fuzz and villains call a police sta-tion. In this case, the factory is in Poland Street, and the central character is a nameless detective working for Unexplained Deaths. The detective, haunted by an insane wife who killed their child, is a moral man who wants to right the wrongs he sees. To him, being a policeman is a vocation, not a job. He ignores the conventions of policing and police procedurals, by investigating the emotions and backgrounds of the victims, both living and dead. He allows himself to feel for them, to be hurt by what happens to them. In the end, the Detective is so overwhelmed by the injustice of the world, that he takes the law into his own hands.

He Died With His Eyes Open (1984) begins with Staniland, a nobody, found dead. He is forgotten by all but the Detective Sergeant. Listening to tapes of the dead man baring his soul, the DS eventually offers his life in exchange for justice. Derek shows us how the dead lived, and what we missed by not taking notice of them when they were alive. In *The Crust On Its Uppers*, Robin glorifies the villains and makes them the heroes, whereas the Factory novels concentrate on the victims. It's almost as if he is paying back for all the terrible things that he has done. Did he feel that way? "... Yes. I think I do...I think I do. I think it's the difference between being 30 when I wrote *Crust*, and being 50 when I wrote *He Died With His Eyes Open*. In the intervening 20 years, you change your way of looking at things. It's increased experience. And growing older. Yep. You think 'hello, time's running out here' and your viewpoint changes."

In *The Devil's Home On Leave* (1985) a horrific killer (ex-Army, chucked out of Belfast, boils his victims in a big vat) is on the loose with connections to a foreign intelligence agency. The case is in the hands of the Detective Sergeant, but he becomes more and more embroiled in events which are too hot to handle. A good but not great book. It was followed by *How The Dead Live* (1986), in which the Detective Sergeant goes to Wiltshire for a spot of detecting. All is not as cosy as one might first suspect. The voices and settings are brooding and mysterious, but it lacks sparkle.

Robin took the face of a dead, anonymous girl in a police photograph, christened her Dora and wrote *I Was Dora Suarez* (1990). It "was my atonement for 50 years' indifference to the miserable state of this world." The Detective Sergeant reads Dora's notebook, and comes to love her. The killer is totally out of control. This is one of the great books of Noir fiction. The opening chapter of *I Was Dora Suarez* has a horrific description of a murder. "There's nothing pretty about murder." In fact, when Robin submitted it, the editor got sick all over the manuscript. "He made a frightful mess of it, actually." He changed publishers.

To Robin, murder is "obscene. If you'd been at the scene of a murder that's the one word you'd use to describe it. You'd say it was obscene. It's reality. It's true, fuck it. I don't know why people think I shouldn't write this sort of stuff. It happens all the time. Just pick up a newspaper. I think it's obscene, so I bloody well say so. Forgive me for getting hot under the collar. Everything in the book is true. It's based on three different cases. What the killer does to his private parts happened. The stuff about the rats going up people's arse-holes is true. It's obscene. It's true."

Robin had personal encounters with psychos. "I had a gun pulled on me once. A little black hole staring at me. The psycho holding it said it wouldn't hurt. I wouldn't feel a thing. 'Not unless he misses,' I thought. That's black, isn't it? Not exactly Mickey Mouse, is it?" And he had his own theories about psychos. "Psycho killers are bores, without imagination. You can't have a killer with a sense of humour. They're boring people. Egotists. Humourless. Though there is a horribly funny side to murder, as a matter of fact - as long as it isn't your own - because, apart from Jack The Ripper, I have never heard of a killer with a single spark of humour.

"I've spent much of my life studying bores, and I've come to the conclusion that the bore bears a close relationship with the assassin. Study of the first forms a base for the study of the second. I don't see how any examination of the Black novel could be complete unless the tell-tale dullness of the killer and the bore were not considered side by side. The bore and the killer are both engaged in the blind pursuit of power - power is the best shield that the disordered personality can conceive against being revealed as the laughing stock that he secretly suspects himself to be. The greatest danger the bore represents is that he makes a beeline for public life."

Robin returned to North London in the 1990s, and took up residence in the Coach & Horses pub on Greek Street, where he extolled the virtues and vices of the Black novel which, in a letter, he once described to me as something 'which you might compare to the feeling a man has in a downward express lift on the 33rd floor when he hears someone above him cutting the cables.' In a very productive period, Robin wrote: an autobiography, *The Hidden Files* (1992); another Factory novel *Dead Man Upright* (1993, the DS talks to an alcoholic ex-copper who thinks there's a 60-year-old serial killer living on the top floor of his block of flats. When the DS stops laughing, he realises his mate may be right...); and a non-series book *Not Till The*

Red Fog Rises (1994). He died peacefully in his sleep, of cancer, on July 30 1994.

"Why do people write books? The error has crept in that the reason is to tell a story, whereas anyone who has ever read real literature knows perfectly well that the reason is also to try as well as the author can to tell the truth."

Signature

This is just a sample. There are many more Noir writers worth considering, including Michael Fessier (*Fully Dressed And In His Right Mind* (1935)), John Lodwick (*Brother Death* (1948)), Elliott Chaze (*Black Wings Has My Angel* (1953)), Harry Crews (*The Gospel Singer* (1968)), Jerome Charyn (*Blue Eyes* (1975)), Paul Auster (City Of Glass (1985)), Andrew Vachss (*Flood* (1985)), Lawrence Block (*When The Sacred Ginmill Closes* (1986)) and the list goes on...

Noir Fiction writers are still morally outraged - Andrew Vachss rages against paedophilia, Harry Crews against hypocrisy in modern society. Noir Fiction writers are still fascinated by the immobilised men, by murder, by death. The characters are still desperate. Still lost in the dark highways of their minds. They still gamble with their lives. They continue to play the black. And we know it will turn up red.

Bang, it is dawn. I open my curtain and see that it is light outside. I have made it through the night.

I know there are more nights to come.

Resource Materials

Reference Books

The Big Book Of Noir ed Ed Gorman, Lee Server & Martin H Greenberg, Carroll & Graf, 1998 A great big book divided into sections: Film, Books, Comics, Radio & Television. Immensely readable and a great range of articles, but it still is not comprehensive. Features Woolrich, Lion Books, Série Noire, Highsmith, Himes, Willeford and more. Highly recommended.

Blues Of A Lifetime: The Autobiography Of Cornell Woolrich, ed Mark T Bassett, Popular Press, 1991 This is an excellent book, full of emotion. The first chapter deals with Woolrich's decision to write his first novel in 1925, the second with his first love in 1923, the third with his Depression experiences in 1933, the fourth is set in his hotel room in 1954 just before his mother's death, and the final fragment is a whimsical piece set in the 1960s.

Cain by Roy Hoopes, Holt RinehartWinston, 1982 A biography of James M Cain. Easy to read, understand and digest. If only all biographies were written so smoothly.

Camus by Herbert R Lottman, Weidenfeld & Nicholson, 1979 The biography that puts all the others to shame. Lottman cuts through the half-truths to read the papers and interview the people first-hand. His recreation of the times is also extremely informative.

Cornell Woolrich: First You Dream, Then You Die by Francis M Nevins, Mysterious Press, 1988 An enormous book which is tedious in the extreme to read because Nevins insists on saying where every idea came from, and how many times it was used. This means that Woolrich's life story does not flow. The best way to approach the book is as a reference tool. There are mistakes, but the copious appendices will provide hours of fun.

Difficult Lives by James Sallis, Gryphon Publications, 1993 A great little book by Noir writer James Sallis consisting of 3 long articles on Jim Thompson, David Goodis and Chester Himes. I would argue that his Goodis piece is the best thing written on Goodis in English. Published at $12.00 by Gryphon Publications, PO Box 209, Brooklyn, NY 11228-0209, USA.

Fyodor Dostoyevsky: A Writer's Life by Geir Kjetsaa (trans Siri Hustvedt & David McDuff), Viking Penguin, 1987 By far the best biography of Dostoyevsky I have read. Kjetsaa has done all the tough research, taking nothing for granted and coming up with what I think is the most accurate portrait of Dostoyevsky's life in print.

Hardboiled America by Geoffrey O'Brien, Van Nostrand, 1981 An excellent early book on vintage US paperbacks, concentrating on Hard-Boiled fiction, but mentioning Thompson, Goodis, Woolrich along the way. Worth getting hold of it for the cover reproductions. It was recently reprinted.

Into The Badlands by John Williams, Paladin, 1991 Excellent combination of travel writing and interview - Williams captures the ambience of both the places and the crime authors who write about them. As well as Ellroy and Vachss, there are 12 other Hard-Boiled contemporary crime novelists to enjoy.

Jim Thompson: Sleep With The Devil by Michael J McCauley, Mysterious Press, 1991 Although not as good as *Savage Art*, this book has a few interesting things to say about Thompson.

Joseph Conrad: A Critical Biography by Jocelyn Baines, Weidenfeld & Nicholson, 1960 Of the half dozen or so books I have on Conrad, I find this one to be the most useful and interesting. Copious excerpts from his correspondence plus considered insights make it a joy to read.

Landmarks In Russian Literature by Maurice Baring, Methuen, 1910 This book contains one of the clearest and most concise essays on Dostoyevsky that I have read.

The Light Went Out by Bruce Hamilton, Constable, 1972 A biography of Patrick Hamilton by his brother Bruce (a novelist in his own right). A very brave book, in that Bruce tries to portray honestly his brother's emotional problems.

Mr Blue: Memoirs Of A Renegade by Edward Bunker, No Exit Press, 1999 A most excellent book in which Bunker recounts important incidents in his life. It is written like fiction - Bunker is telling the story of his life, not slavishly recounting details - and it is all the better for it.

Nathanael West: The Art Of His Life by Jay Martin, Farrar, Strauss & Giroux, 1970 A great biography of a writer who died far too young. Contains many previously unpublished extracts from West's papers.

Neon Noir by Woody Haut, Serpent's Tail, 1999, ISBN 1-85242-547-4, £10.99 A very good survey of contemporary US crime fiction, taking us through the major writers from Kennedy's assassination to the present day. I could quibble with its lack of certain writers but hey, let us be grateful it exists at all. Noir writers covered include Thompson, Willeford, Sallis and Ellroy.

Patrick Hamilton: A Life by Sean French, Faber & Faber, 1993 Good solid biography.

Pulp Culture by Woody Haut, Serpent's Tail, 1995, ISBN 1-85242-319-6, £9.99 Haut's book on 'Hard Boiled Fiction & The Cold War' spends a lot of time on Goodis, Himes, Thompson and Willeford. Haut is very well read on the major authors, but fails to put the genre into context re: their 1930s roots. Still, well worth picking up.

Savage Art: A Biography Of Jim Thompson by Robert Polito, Serpent's Tail, 1997, ISBN 1-85242-571-7, £15.00 As thorough and comprehensive as his research is, Polito has the habit of making every little incident in Thompson's life SIGNIFICANT and, at the same time, an important influence on his work. This is annoying. I wish biographers would stop doing that. Besides this irritation, an excellent, detailed biography.

The Third Degree: Crime Writers In Conversation by Paul Duncan, No Exit Press, 1997, ISBN 1-874061-85-8, £7.99 Features long interviews with 4 Noir writers (Edward Bunker, James Ellroy, Derek Raymond, James Sallis) and 11 other mystery writers (Patricia Cornwell, Lawrence Block, etc.).

Through A Glass Darkly: The Life Of Patrick Hamilton by Nigel Jones, Scribners, 1991 Of the 3 Hamilton biographies, the one I enjoyed the most.

Tough Guy Writers Of The Thirties edited by David Madden, Southern Illinois University Press, 1968 One of the best reference books in my collection, this is a series of articles about Noir and Hard-Boiled writers including Cain, Gresham, Thompson. McCoy and Eric Knight/Richard Hallas.

Willeford by Don Herron, Dennis McMillan, 1997 Almost 300 pages of text about Willeford's life, 100 pages of conversation with Willeford, and almost 100 pages listing everything he had published. Sometimes annoyingly pedantic but, more often than not, Willeford's personality shines through. Indispensable.

Magazines

Crime Time 2, Feb 1996, includes *Hollywood & Bust* by Paul Buck (about Horace McCoy).

Crime Time 3, April 1996, includes *The Search For Otis* by Gary Lovisi (about Lion Books author G H Otis).

Crime Time 5, Aug 1996, includes *Gold Medal Days* by Ed Gorman (includes Goodis & Thompson).

Crime Time 9, 1997, includes *The Fragile Fist Of Charles Willeford* by Paul Duncan.

Crime Time 10, 1997, includes *An Introduction To Isaac Sidel* by Peter Walker (about Jerome Charyn).

Crime Time 2.1, 1998, includes *Life's A Bitch* by Eddie Duggan (about Goodis).

Crime Time 2.3, 1998, includes *It's Raining Violence: A Brief History Of British Noir* by Paul Duncan (Not so brief and, to be honest, more Hard-Boiled than Noir).

Crime Time 2.4, 1999, includes *Gerald Kersh: Soho (1929-1938)* by Paul Duncan, *James Sallis, Allusionism And Play* by Richard Martin.

Crime Time 2.5, 1999, includes *Cigarettes & Alcohol: Jim Thompson* by Charles Waring, and *The Last Word On Noir* (two articles, one by Woody Haut about his book *Neon Noir*, one by Paul Duncan).

Crime Time 2.6, 1999, includes *Writing In Darkness: The World Of Cornell Woolrich* by Eddie Duggan.

David Goodis/Pulps Pictured, BFI, 32-page magazine issued to coincide with Goodis film tour. Contains articles about the author as well as the films.

Firsts, March 2000, *Gerald Kersh: Man Of Many Skins* by Paul Duncan, a survey of his novels.

Other Words, December 1988, includes *No Holds Barred* by Jeb Nichols (about James Curtis).

Paperback Parade 15, Oct 1989, Special Noir Issue includes *An Interview With Arnold Hano* by George Tuttle (Hano edited Lion Books who published Thompson, Karp and Goodis among other Noir writers), *Jim Thompson's Vision Of The Paradoxically Evil Mess* and *And I Still Haven't Got Him Out Of My Mind* by Charles Culpepper (both about Thompson), and more on Film Noir.

Paperback Parade 21, Nov 1990, includes *A Talk With Barry Gifford* by Tom Cantrell (Gifford talks about his Black Lizard imprint).

Paperback Parade 33, Mar 1993 Special Gold Medal Issue includes articles about Gold Medal and an interview with editor Knox Burger. Gold Medal published Goodis, Thompson and other Noir writers.

Paperback, Pulp & Comic Collector 3, 1991, includes *P J Wolfson* by Paul Buck.

Paperbacks, Pulps & Comics Volume 3, 1995, includes *David Goodis: Poet Of The Losers* by Dave Moore.

Readercon 11 Souvenir Book, 1999, Articles about Gerald Kersh by Paul Duncan and Jim Sallis, an introduction by Harlan Ellison, and a full bibliography by Paul Duncan.

Anthologies

The Arbor House Treasury Of Detective & Mystery Stories From The Great Pulps ed Bill Pronzini, Priam Books, 1983 A collection of 15 stories from *Black Mask*, *Dime Detective* and other pulps including McCoy, Woolrich and others. As well as an introduction, there is biographical material on each writer.

Black Lizard Anthology Of Crime Fiction, ed Ed Gorman, Black Lizard, 1987 Includes stories by Jim Thompson, Joe Lansdale, James Reasoner, Ed Gorman, Harlan Ellison, Harry Whittington.

The Black Mask Boys by William F Nolan, Mysterious Press, 1987 A definitive, fascinating book which is both a history, an appreciation and a sampler of *Black Mask* magazine, the pulp where Hard-Boiled began. Features Carroll John Daly, Dashiell Hammett, Raoul Whitfield, Frederick Nebel, Horace McCoy, Paul Cain, Raymond Chandler.

Hard-Boiled, ed Bill Pronzini & Jack Adrian, Oxford University Press, 1995 Includes stories by Cain, Himes, Goodis, Thompson, Vachss, Ellroy & Gorman. One of the best of the recent collections because as well as the excellent short stories, Pronzini and Adrian have included informative introductions to each featured writer.

London Noir, ed Maxim Jakubowski, Serpent's Tail, 1994 Includes a story by Derek Raymond. The other authors are not really Noir but have a good try.

Internet

Noir Webring - www.webring.org/cgi-bin/webring?ring=noirweb;list - This ring has a long list of Noir (and not so Noir) sites. Peruse at your leisure.

Cain/Gresham - www.lib.umd.edu/UMCP/RARE/797hmpgf.html - This University of Maryland site shows different hardback and paperback editions of James M Cain and William Lindsay Gresham. Not much text.

James Sallis – www.jamessallis.com – Superb collection of interviews, articles, short stories etc assembled by Richard Martin.

Dennis McMillan Publications - www.booksellers.com/dmp - Not only does Dennis McMillan sell great books (Charles Willeford, James Crumley, Kent Anderson), but he and wife Maura have put together one of the best, most informative sites I have seen. There are many pages on Charles Willeford and other writers.

The Nights And Cities Of Gerald Kersh – www.harlanellison.com/kersh – Article, bibliography and reviews about this rediscovered author.

Thrilling Detective - www.colba.net/~kvnsmith/thrillingdetective/trivia/detlinks.html - A great site to find out about private eyes, but it also has many great Hard-Boiled/Noir links. Edited by Kevin Burton Smith.

Rara Avis Newsgroup - Highly recommended Hard-Boiled/Noir mailing list monitored by William Denton. Always interesting. Always controversial. Full of writers, editors, agents and readers who are all fans of the genre. To get the digest version send message 'subscribe rara-avis-digest' to majordomo@icomm.ca. To look at the archives, go to: www.miskatonic.org/rara-avis

The AOL Hardboiled Bulletin Board - If you belong to America On-line, enter the keyword Books, and then go to chats and bulletin boards and then to the mystery community, etc.

The Essential Library: Film Best-Sellers

Build up your library with new titles every month

Film Noir by Paul Duncan

The laconic private eye, the corrupt cop, the heist that goes wrong, the femme fatale with the rich husband and the dim lover - these are the trademark characters of Film Noir. This book charts the progression of the Noir style as a vehicle for film-makers who wanted to record the darkness at the heart of American society as it emerged from World War to the Cold War. As well as an introduction explaining the origins of Film Noir, seven films are examined in detail and an exhaustive list of over 500 Films Noirs are listed.

Alfred Hitchcock (Revised & Updated Edition) by Paul Duncan

More than 20 years after his death, Alfred Hitchcock is still a household name, most people in the Western world have seen at least one of his films, and he popularised the action movie format we see every week on the cinema screen. He was both a great artist and dynamite at the box office. This book examines the genius and enduring popularity of one of the most influential figures in the history of the cinema!

Orson Welles (Revised & Updated Edition) by Martin Fitzgerald

The popular myth is that after the artistic success of *Citizen Kane* it all went downhill for Orson Welles, that he was some kind of fallen genius. Yet, despite overwhelming odds, he went on to make great Films Noirs like *The Lady From Shanghai* and *Touch Of Evil*. He translated Shakespeare's work into films with heart and soul (*Othello, Chimes At Midnight, Macbeth*), and he gave voice to bitterness, regret and desperation in *The Magnificent Ambersons* and *The Trial*. Far from being down and out, Welles became one of the first cutting-edge independent film-makers.

Woody Allen (Revised & Updated Edition) by Martin Fitzgerald

Woody Allen: Neurotic. Jewish. Funny. Inept. Loser. A man with problems. Or so you would think from the characters he plays in his movies. But hold on. Allen has written and directed 30 films. He may be a funny man, but he is also one of the most serious American film-makers of his generation. This revised and updated edition includes *Sweet And Lowdown* and *Small Time Crooks*.

Stanley Kubrick (Revised & Updated Edition) by Paul Duncan

Kubrick's work, like all masterpieces, has a timeless quality. His vision is so complete, the detail so meticulous, that you believe you are in a three-dimensional space displayed on a two-dimensional screen. He was commercially successful because he embraced traditional genres like War (*Paths Of Glory, Full Metal Jacket*), Crime (*The Killing*), Science Fiction (*2001*), Horror (*The Shining*) and Love (*Barry Lyndon*). At the same time, he stretched the boundaries of film with controversial themes: underage sex (*Lolita*); ultra violence (*A Clockwork Orange*); and erotica (*Eyes Wide Shut*).

The Essential Library: Currently Available

Film Directors:

Woody Allen (2nd)	**Tim Burton**	**Ang Lee**
Jane Campion*	**John Carpenter**	**Joel & Ethan Coen (2nd)**
Jackie Chan	**Steven Soderbergh**	**Clint Eastwood**
David Cronenberg	**Terry Gilliam***	**Michael Mann**
Alfred Hitchcock (2nd)	**Krzysztof Kieslowski***	**Roman Polanski**
Stanley Kubrick (2nd)	**Sergio Leone**	**Oliver Stone**
David Lynch (2nd)	**Brian De Palma***	**George Lucas**
Sam Peckinpah*	**Ridley Scott (2nd)**	**James Cameron**
Orson Welles (2nd)	**Billy Wilder**	**Roger Corman**
Steven Spielberg	**Mike Hodges**	**Spike Lee**
Hal Hartley		

Film Genres:

Blaxploitation Films	**Bollywood**	**French New Wave**
Horror Films	**Spaghetti Westerns**	**Vietnam War Movies**
Slasher Movies	**Film Noir**	**Hammer Films**
Vampire Films*	**Heroic Bloodshed***	**Carry On Films**
German Expressionist Films		

Film Subjects:

Laurel & Hardy	**Marx Brothers**	**Film Music**
Steve McQueen*	**Marilyn Monroe**	**The Oscars® (2nd)**
Filming On A Microbudget	**Bruce Lee**	**Writing A Screenplay**
Film Studies		

Music:

The Madchester Scene	**Beastie Boys**	**Jethro Tull**
How To Succeed In The Music Business		**The Beatles**

Literature:

Cyberpunk	**Philip K Dick**	**The Beat Generation**
Agatha Christie	**Sherlock Holmes**	**Noir Fiction**
Terry Pratchett	**Hitchhiker's Guide (2nd)**	**Alan Moore**
William Shakespeare	**Creative Writing**	**Tintin**
Georges Simenon		

Ideas:

Conspiracy Theories	**Nietzsche**	**UFOs**
Feminism	**Freud & Psychoanalysis**	**Bisexuality**

History:

Alchemy & Alchemists	**The Crusades**	**The Black Death**
Jack The Ripper	**The Rise Of New Labour**	**Ancient Greece**
American Civil War	**American Indian Wars**	**Witchcraft**
Globalisation	**Who Shot JFK?**	**Nuclear Paranoia**

Miscellaneous:

Stock Market Essentials	**How To Succeed As A Sports Agent**	**Doctor Who**
Classic Radio Comedy	**Videogaming**	

Available at bookstores or send a cheque (payable to 'Oldcastle Books') to: **Pocket Essentials (Dept NF2), P O Box 394, Harpenden, Herts, AL5 1XJ, UK**. £3.99 each (£2.99 if marked with an *). For each book add 50p(UK)/£1 (elsewhere) postage & packing